Contents

Introduction

Surfing's popularity has sky-rocketed in the last 20 years, with thousands of beach-goers now taking to the waves. It's a unique, challenging sport to partake in, and the surroundings are often breathtaking. Be warned, though – surfing is totally addictive, and once you start, you might well find that it takes over your life!

Surfing began in ancient Polynesia, where it was part of spiritual belief. In Hawaii, it became known as the sport of kings because royalty rode the biggest and best boards, however, it wasn't only the boys – women were also a part of the wave-riding tradition! Although subdued by the coming of missionaries and Christianity, surfing never died. It spread with the coming of the explorer Captain Cook and, with the advent of wetsuits and modern surfboard-making techniques, since the 1960s it has become a sport, lifestyle and culture all of its own. Fascinating, complex and sometimes intimidating, the world of surfing provides thousands of people with a living and a lifestyle as well as a fun, healthy sport.

'The cure for anything is salt water; sweat, tears, or the sea.'

Isak Dinesen, pen name of Karen Blixen, 1885-1962.

> 'Where there is a very great sea and surf breaking on the shore, they lay themselves upon an oval piece of plank. They wait the time of the greatest swell and push forward with their arms. It sends them in with a most astonishing velocity, and the great art is to guide the plank so as always to keep it in a proper direction on top of the swell.'
>
> Lieutenant James King, who wrote the world's first description of surfing on his voyage to Hawaii with Captain Cook.

Is surfing easy to learn?

Yes and no! Surfing is one of the most difficult sports to excel at, but it is still hugely satisfying at any level. The basics can be picked up in one lesson, with many beginners standing and riding a wave to the shore the first day they try. The exhilaration of this feeling keeps surfers coming back for more and more.

But it takes a lot more time to become a good surfer, because no two waves are the same – you can't practise a move until the right kind of wave comes along, unlike say skateboarding, where you can fly over the same kerb again and again until you get your ollies right. The water is moving, the board is moving, you're moving … and although we all came from the sea, we are now land dwellers, and learning how the ocean moves and flows is a task in itself. This book aims to give you the basics, so you can be confident in your approach to the sport of kings.

What do I need to know?

Basic safety and ocean knowledge is paramount. Surfing is pretty safe, as long as you are sensible and learn the rules of the ocean. If you have a reasonable level of fitness and a bit of determination, you can be enjoying yourself in a very short time. Reading this book will give you the basics, and going to a surf school will solidify the essential knowledge.

You also need to know how to predict when the waves will come, what kinds of waves there are, what equipment you need and how to ride your first waves.

How do I get started?

Once you have read this book, the best way to get going is to have a lesson or two at a good surf school, there are loads in the UK. Then you can hire equipment and continue the learning process until you know you're hooked – that's when you get grumpy if you haven't been surfing for a week or so! Then it's time to buy your own gear (see chapter 1) and start setting out on your own surf trips.

Is it expensive?

Once you have a board and wetsuit (a few hundred quid's worth at least, or about a tenner if you're hiring), everything else is pretty much free. Car parking charges are often all you'll have to pay for your hours in the sea! The freedom and relative simplicity of the sport are one of its major draws. What surfing gives back to you in terms of health, happiness and an increased awareness of the beautiful world we live in, pays any initial investment back in spades!

Disclaimer

The ocean is an unpredictable place which can prove very dangerous. Make sure you are a competent swimmer, know the basic rules of the beach and don't go out of your comfort zone while you are learning. Always listen to the lifeguards.

Chapter One

Equipment

Once you've got a board and wetsuit, you can have endless hours of free fun on the beach. This chapter is a rundown of the basic kit you will need, and what to pick to suit your surfing.

Types of boards

- Soft boards are the blue or yellow 'banana' foam boards most surf schools use. They're stable and won't knock you out if they hit you on the head. They cost about £150.

- Pop-outs or moulded boards are made by filling a fibreglass mould with polyurethane foam. They're heavier but last longer – ideal once you're past soft boards. You can pick one up second-hand for about £100 if you're lucky.

- Epoxy boards produced by companies like Surftech, NSP and Resin8 and are gaining popularity. The foam is often machine-shaped and is then encased in an epoxy shell. Epoxy boards are lighter, tougher and more environmentally friendly. They tend to surf better in small waves than their polyester resin cousins as they are more floaty.

- The most popular type of board, custom boards are made by hand from foam blanks, which these days are often roughly shaped by a machine first. A 'shaper' (board maker) finishes the shape, and it's then covered with fibreglass cloth and polyester resin. These boards are more easily damaged, but lighter and more finely-tuned. Suitable for all abilities, you can pick them up from around £150 second-hand, but you'll need to know what you're on about (or take an experienced mate) to avoid picking something up with faults like badly fixed dings. A brand new surfboard will set you back several hundred pounds. Buy a bag for it to reduce dings and sun damage.

Anatomy of a surfboard

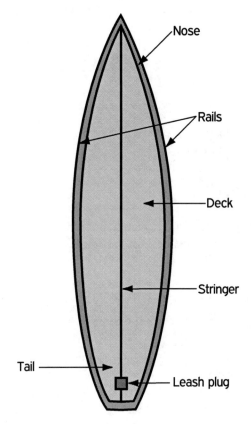

Nose

Rails

Deck

Stringer

Tail

Leash plug

Measurements

Surfboards are measured in feet and inches. A board will often have its measurements written along the stringer on the bottom. The first measurement given when talking about boards is the length (from nose to tail), then comes the width (at the widest point), then the thickness (you might also see nose and tail widths, taken 12in from the ends, not really important unless you're a pro or make surfboards!). The plan shape of the board is what it looks like from above. Most all-round boards will be narrowest at the nose, widest behind the middle and taper to the tail.

Volume is determined by all these measurements, and the volume of your board is very important, especially if you're learning. This is where your own height, weight and the waves you surf come into play. More volume floats you and makes it easier to paddle and catch waves. Too much and you can't duck-dive (move yourself and the board under the waves) and the board will be less manoeuvrable.

Shapes

- Fish – shorter, fatter and wider than the average shortboard. Popular in the summer, these are excellent to ride in small waves, but demand a different riding style which may mean when you hop back onto your regular shortboard, you have to cope with a period of adjustment.

- Shortboard – still the dominant board type, typically from 6-7ft in length, generally with three fins.

- Mini-mal – over 7ft and up to 9ft long with a rounded nose and plenty of width. These are fun in small summer waves.

- Longboard – usually over 9ft in length and 22in, or more, wide with a rounded nose.

- Gun – long and narrow, made for riding huge waves and pretty much useless in any other situation.

- Retro board – all sorts of boards that don't fit into any other category and revisit older design ideas. Almost anything goes.

Features

- Tail shape – tails come in square, round, squash, pin or swallow, but while you're learning you don't need to worry too much about that. The most common shape is a squash tail, which is a combination of the square and round type and gives good all-round performance.

- Rocker – this is the bend in the board from nose to tail; most boards will have a little. More rocker equals more turning ease but the board will be harder to control down the line, i.e. going across the face of the wave. It's a trade-off.

'More volume floats you and makes it easier to paddle and catch waves. Too much and you can't duck-dive (move yourself and the board under the waves) and the board will be less manoeuvrable.'

- Concave – a scoop taken out of the board's bottom, from rail to rail. It's pretty subtle but you can find it by running a hand over the bottom. A concave might be between the fins or more towards the middle of the board. It's pretty standard to have a bit of concave; it creates lift and acceleration.

- Vee – this is less standard in a modern board. The bottom centre point is raised higher than the rail. You'll feel a panel either side of the stringer. It helps a board roll from rail to rail, but can obstruct the flow from nose to tail.

- Rails – can be rounded or 'blocky' for stability, which equals slower and harder to turn, or turned-down, which equals easier to turn but less stable.

- Fins – fins are what keeps your board stuck into the wave. Variations do make a difference, but again, only if you're experienced. Three fin or thruster boards are by far the most common, despite the retro board resurgence. Just make sure you've got at least one fin in there!

'Your first board should be a "foamy" or soft board, whether you hire it on the beach, buy one or use a surf school's. They are ideal to learn on and lots of fun.'

Buying a board

The progression from beginner's board to your perfect steed is full of pitfalls, so read on to avoid getting a board which will hamper your progress. Many shapers will give invaluable hints on their website about board choice, and often have forms or other tools to help you along the path.

First board to full on quiver

Your first board should be a 'foamy' or soft board, whether you hire it on the beach, buy one or use a surf school's. They are ideal to learn on and lots of fun.

Next, you should buy, beg or borrow something nice and floaty like a mini-mal. Keep the volume and length up and you'll progress, if you've decided you want to be a cruisy longboarder, you're set, as they have plenty of both. Get a board at least 12in longer than you are tall, but try to avoid anything too cumbersome – you don't want to be battling the board as this wastes energy.

Make sure you don't buy a skinny little shortboard too soon. Do you want to surf or look cool? You should work your way down in size gradually, or your surfing life will end in frustration. Mini-mals are an excellent way to progress out of the white water and onto real waves once you can stand. Mini-mals are harder to come by second-hand, so if you buy a new one and want to progress to a shorter board in a year or two, you should get a decent amount of money back for it.

Once the mini-mal starts to hold you back (it's not fast enough, you can't duck-dive it out to the bigger waves you want to be on, or it turns too slowly for you), it might be time to start thinking about a shorter board.

Remember to think volume and length. You need it to paddle into waves easily and be stable. Take an experienced friend who knows your surfing level, and be prepared to be very honest with the salespeople or shaper. Get as much advice as you can from any surfing mates or your instructors. Don't be afraid to ask a ton of questions – good salespeople want to sell you a board you love so you'll come back for your next one. Go for something with clean simple lines, nothing fussy, and don't buy something just because you like the spray job!

Try to buy from a reputable brand – the market is being flooded with boards made cheaply in the Far East, but sometimes they aren't quite up to the same standard or made with the same care as your local shaper crafts his boards; he (there are very few female shapers) also has the advantage of knowing local conditions intimately. You'll get a better resale value from something with a good brand name or from a reputable, local shaper.

The shape of the board you choose is up to you. Check out the shapes listed earlier in this chapter and learn to recognise what other people are riding. If you get a chance to try out a mate's board, always say yes as it's a chance to find out what works and what doesn't for your riding.

Board bag

A boardsock is okay if you aren't taking your board far, but for anything else a good bag is worth the money, 60% of dings happen on land! Get one that is padded with a comfortable strap and silver reflective panels to keep your board cool and to stop the wax melting.

Leash

This attaches to a plug at the back of the board at one end, and a Velcro strap attaches to your ankle, or just below the knee if it's a longboard leash. Features can include a padded strap, moulded double swivel (so that you don't get tangled up), a detachable railsaver (a strap that prevents the leash cord damaging your board) and key pocket. Leashes don't vary all that much in price but it is worth getting a good one.

Wax and grip

So that your feet don't slide off the deck of the board, you'll need some wax and probably a tailpad, also known as deck grip. Quite often it's a matter of personal choice, but most people now use wax all over, or wax for the front foot and a tailpad for the back. Wax is cheap, easy and fast to put on and provides good traction, plus it smells nice! A tailpad can help you make sure you've got your back foot in the right place, it will save on wax, lasts longer and protects the deck of the board to some extent. If you're using a pad, follow the application instructions very carefully, as there's nothing worse than having it peel off.

How to wax your board

Choose a block of wax from a reputable brand like Sex Wax or Ocean & Earth. Wax comes in different varieties for different water temperatures, so make sure you choose 'cold' if you are surfing in the UK!

- If you need to get old wax off the board, pour warm (but not too hot!) water over the deck to loosen it, then scrape it off with a wax comb or a card.

- Base coat – some people swear by it, some people don't, so this is up to you.

- Grab your block and make diagonal criss-crosses with the wax over the deck of the board. You need to wax from the leash plug up to where your neck is when you are lying on the board.

- Now rub the wax over the lines in a circular motion. Little humps will begin to build up – this is good! You only need to put on a couple of layers then add a bit more every time you surf.

Don't leave your board in the sun or it'll melt the wax, obviously enough, and it will also turn the board yellow. Don't put your board deck down in the sand either.

Use a wax comb to rough up the deck if the grip factor decreases – drag the teeth diagonally one way, then the other. Keep your wax in a little bag or pot so you can always find some and don't get it covered in sand. When you get to the end of a block, tiny slivers of wax can be saved and melted together so you don't waste any.

Wetsuits

Choose the best wetty you can afford so you're warm enough to surf as long as you want. You need a 3/2mm suit from about May to October in the UK. That's a 3mm thickness of neoprene on the legs and body and 2mm on the areas of most movement, e.g. shoulders. Fit is paramount, followed by stretchiness, but the newer, thinner neoprene doesn't last as long, so bear that in mind. Don't go to Tesco for it – get a made-for-surfers suit, you'll be glad you did!

A wetsuit works by trapping pockets of air in the neoprene to insulate you. They come in different thicknesses for different water temperatures. Some have a zip up the back; some come with a chest zip and overhead barrier – just choose whatever fits best.

'Don't leave your board in the sun or it'll melt the wax, obviously enough, and it will also turn the board yellow. Don't put your board deck down in the sand either.'

Buyer's guide

- Go into the shop with a good idea of the maximum amount of money that you want to spend.
- Make sure you are aware of the terms that refer to wetsuit features so you won't be blinded with jargon by the sales assistant (see overleaf).

- When you've got the suit on, check for baggy areas in the lumbar panel of the back, under the arms and on the back of your knees; there shouldn't be much slack material here.

- Make sure that the neck, wrist and ankles are comfortably tight so that they won't flush (fill with water) or rub.

- Check each of the panels carefully for nicks or pulls in the lining.

- Jump up and down and do a few stretches. The suit should be as tight as you can comfortably bear, and you should not be able to easily pull the neoprene away from your body. The neck will often feel really tight because you are not used to it, but it needs to be tight to keep as much water out as possible.

- If you're not dying of heat exhaustion from trying on tight wetsuits under hot lights, give a few different entry system suits a try – mini zip, back zip, shortened zip and so on.

- Ask about warranty or guarantee, then fill in the card on the purchase tag if needs be.

Wetsuit terminology

- Hollow fibre – heat retaining fibre, some with water resistant coating. The hollow fibre retains body heat, while repelling and wicking water away from the body. It goes under trade names such as 'Dry max' or 'Plush'.

- Zip closures – Y-flap, batwing, total closure: whatever they're called, they stop zip flush. Combined with collars they seal the suit and reduce flushing.

- Low-friction collar – wetsuit rub around the neck used to be a problem every surfer suffered, but the new low-friction materials such as Glideskin and Lycra not only increase comfort but also sit closely against the skin preventing water entry.

- Smooth skins, mesh skins – all updated versions of the single-skin neoprene which reduces the cooling effect of water evaporating off the suit, thus fighting wind-chill.

- Liquid seams, fluid weld – basically a high-tech glue finish on a seam. The idea is to reduce stitching because it restricts a suit's flexibility.

- Super-stretch neoprene – great in the right places. Make sure your suit has the finest available as low-end, super-flex neoprene has a reduced memory, i.e. it stretches and doesn't return to its original shape.

- Knee pads – used to be the first place a wetsuit would wear, so manufacturers stuck great chunks of plastic on there. Nowadays there are no end of resin finishes and pads that are comfortable and effective.

- Fit – the most important factor. Even though modern suits are mega-flexy and tend to fit a wider array of shapes and sizes, it's still important to try on suits. Most differ in cut, with differing lengths of body, arms and legs. If a suit is too tight it will reduce the insulating effect of the neoprene. Too loose and you'll flush with cold water, not nice!

Wetsuit facts that the shop assistant may forget to tell you:

- The more seams there are, the less stretchy the suit will be (and the more funny marks you'll have left on your skin when you peel it off!).

- Single-lined neoprene (that's the 'slick' stuff) is less hardwearing than double-lined.

- Velcro fasteners damage double-lined material so beware of too much fastening around the neck.

- A Lycra rash vest does not make you warmer, it just prevents rash.

- A summer suit will usually be warm enough from the middle of May until the middle of October; even with a thermal rash vest it will not be warm enough to surf in the UK year round.

'Even though modern suits are mega-flexy and tend to fit a wider array of shapes and sizes, it's still important to try on suits.'

Wetsuit accessories

When it gets too much for the extremities and you've moved into your winter suit, you'll also need some booties, a hood and some gloves.

- Gloves – some people can go without gloves, but you're risking early arthritis – get a good pair and they'll help, not hinder, your paddling.

- Booties – make sure these fit like, um, a glove, or you'll have the dreaded folded-over-boot-toe which is inevitably followed by the head-over-heels dismount. Most people swear by split-toe boots, which give you more of a feel of the board under your feet.

- Hood – not attractive and not fun to wear, but they protect your ears. Get one that doesn't strangle you but is tight enough to prevent flush. The best ones are built into wetties or rash vests – less chance of flushing down the back.

- Rash vests – a thermal rashy can give you extra warmth around your vital internal organs. If your core is warm, you can keep surfing for longer.

- Earplugs – prolonged exposure to cold water and the wind can result in surfer's ear, where the bone in the inner ear grows over. Trapped water is painful, can cause infections and you'll need an operation if the condition get bad. Wear earplugs to avoid this and a hood when it's really cold.

'A ding is what surfers call damage to a surfboard. The most basic kind of ding repair kit is a simple tube of premixed resin like the Ocean & Earth Solacure kit.'

Ding repair

A ding is what surfers call damage to a surfboard. The most basic kind of ding repair kit is a simple tube of premixed resin like the Ocean & Earth Solacure kit.

Here's how to fix a small ding:

- Make sure the ding is dry – water left in the board will cause havoc (delamination, discolouration, opening up of the repair, yuk!). A couple of days in a warm room will do it.

- Clean and dry around the ding.

- Use a bit of sandpaper to rough up the edges and blunt any sharp ones. For larger dings, you may need to cut away some of the area to tidy it up, and use foam or fibreglass cloth to fill it up. Get rid of the dust.

- Squeeze resin mix onto the area (do this out of direct sunlight).

- Spread evenly with an ice-lolly stick or similar.

- Expose to direct sunlight.

- You should be able to sand it down after about half an hour, then get back in the water!

Delamination is when the deck comes away from the foam blank underneath. It's characterised by soft squashy patches and often discolouration. Solacure doesn't give the most professional finish, but it gets you back in the water fast.

One step up is a proper ding repair kit. Seabase sell these online (see help list) and in most surf shops; the pack looks like a margarine tub. You get everything you need – resin and hardener, fibreglass cloth, sandpaper and so on – even little tubs to mix the gloop. There's also a full set of instructions, but if you want more information or you've got some serious dings, *The Ding Repair Scriptures* (Village Green Publications) is widely recognised as the Bible of ding repair advice. Resin is expensive, but never cut corners by buying resin made for repairing scratches on cars – the nasty yellow colour will devalue any board it touches!

You should always have a repair kit when you travel, and keep one at home as well. If you add a fin key, leash and leash string, wax and spare fins and you've pretty much got a full emergency kit.

'You should always have a repair kit when you travel, and keep one at home as well. If you add a fin key, leash and leash string, wax and spare fins and you've pretty much got a full emergency kit.'

Checklist – what you need for a typical UK surf trip

The omission of any one of these things can make for a miserable surf, so get into the habit of keeping your gear clean and together so it's easy to grab pre-session.

Essential	Non-essential
Surfboard(s)	Boots, gloves and hood (in winter)
Wax	Rash vest
Leash	Board shorts
Swimsuit	Extra warm clothes for aprés surf
Wetsuit	Car park money
Towel	Earplugs
Bag or box for wet gear	Ding repair kit
Boots, gloves and hood	Wax comb

Summing Up

- Check out www.second-handboards.com and eBay to see what sort of boards are out there.

- Find your nearest surf shop and head over there to see what kind of equipment they have on offer.

- Also have a look at online surf shops and shaper websites – they give tons of board and wetsuit advice.

- If you have a chance to check out other people's boards, run your hands over the rails and the bottom (particularly between the fins) to see if you can suss out the contours. Ask the owner – they'll probably be very happy to talk about their favourite board!

- Try on as many wetties as you can bear to and formulate an idea of what you want to buy.

Chapter Two

How Waves Work

Not all waves are created equal, and picking the right conditions to surf in will make the difference between a good and bad session, between learning to surf at a reasonable pace or struggling to ever get to your feet. Ocean knowledge is something that is best learnt through practical experience – getting out there, watching the ocean and immersing yourself in it. However, that's not always possible, so you can begin by gaining an understanding of some of the basic ocean processes – how waves are formed, how they break and what different kinds of waves and surfing locations ('breaks') there are.

First up, waves come in sets and lulls. A set of waves is a group of waves, typically between four and seven to a group, which break on the beach. This is followed by a lull or a break in waves, which can be five minutes or 15 (hopefully not more), where the waves are smaller and you have the chance to paddle back and get ready for the next set! The conditions you are looking for is a nice groundswell which produces clear sets and lulls.

Forecasting swell

It's a common misconception that a windy day means good surf. Wind does create the waves, but ideally it wants to be blowing hard over a long fetch (area) of the ocean for as long as possible and as far away from your break as possible. Small wavelets whipped up by the wind (windswell), eventually become larger waves which run together into rideable sets of waves which we call 'groundswell'. Ocean swells move at 20-25mph, so a swell generated by a low pressure area in the mid-Atlantic will typically take three or four days to arrive on UK beaches. Local winds mess up the waves, but they can also generate rideable windswell waves which are less organised than groundswell but can still be fun.

'Wind does create the waves, but ideally it wants to be blowing hard over a long fetch (area) of the ocean for as long as possible and as far away from your break as possible.'

If you want to know when there are going to be good waves, there are loads of resources out there. Websites like www.magicseaweed.co.uk allow you to select the beach nearest to you and see a rating for the surf in the coming week. This makes life easy, but simplistic 'four out of five stars' predictions may sometimes steer you wrong, so you should learn to read synoptic weather charts for yourself.

The most useful Internet charts are the ones which show animated predictions for the next few days based on the Wave Amplitude Model (WAM charts). Study each chart then watch them run through to see how the swell develops and its direction. You're looking for low pressure systems with tightly packed isobars (those are the lines on the map – the closer the bars are together, the stronger the wind). The wind blows anticlockwise and parallel to the isobars in a low pressure system. The numbers represent the atmospheric pressure in millibars – anything under 1,000 means a low pressure swell generator. High pressure systems create sunny, calm weather and don't really generate swell.

It's ideal to have a low pressure system tracking across the Atlantic towards the UK with a high pressure system sitting over the country to create good weather and light offshore winds on the western coasts (winds rotate in a clockwise direction around highs).

Have a look at the image opposite for a perfect example. This shows a deep low pressure system. The black arrow (on the left) shows the area where swell is being generated, and the direction it's travelling in. This low, if it was in the mid-Atlantic, would produce a southwest swell, heading straight for Devon, Cornwall, Wales and southwest Ireland. It should also provide waves for the Channel Islands and the south coast. If there was an area of high pressure over Britain, the result would be offshore winds in most areas, giving classic surfing conditions.

Once you've identified a good forecast, how do you know if the swell has hit your break? If you're going to be driving miles to get there, you need to know in advance that it's worth it. Check any webcams that are nearby and ring anyone who can tell you. You can also check the buoy readings and the local wind reports to give you a good idea of what's going on locally. Find your nearest buoy on www.ndbc.noaa.gov. The readings you're interested in are the windspeed, dominant wave period (how far apart the waves are) and wave height.

> 'The most useful Internet charts are the ones which show animated predictions for the next few days based on the Wave Amplitude Model (WAM charts).'

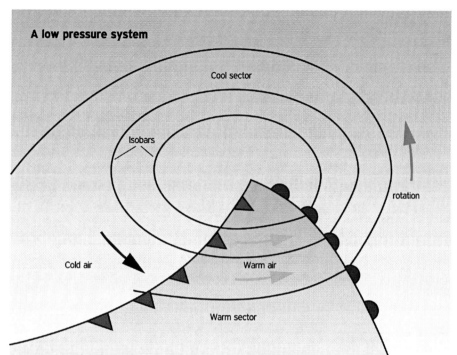

A low pressure system

Cool sector

Isobars

rotation

Cold air

Warm air

Warm sector

A decent wave period is 8 or more – anything above 10 is lovely. This means the waves have organised themselves into groundswell, nicely spaced apart. Periods of less than 7 means locally-generated messy windswell. You want the winds to be as light as possible and preferably offshore. Check the wave height too – you need to know what works for your beach, and remember that a height of 20ft is the height at the buoy – it won't be that big on the beach! Look at the previous readings and you will see how the swell has built over time. Different beaches and areas will work with different combinations, and it takes time to learn what works for you.

By knowing the basics of surf forecasting, checking the charts and using Internet forecasting sites and mobile apps wisely, you'll up your hit rate and never miss a session.

If you want to learn more about the science of waves, you can't go wrong with *Surf Science* by Dr Tony Butt.

There are lots of swell-chasing websites listed in the help list, some of the more well-known ones are www.magicseaweed.co.uk, www.windguru.com and www. A1Surf.com.

Tides

The tides of the ocean are caused by the moon, which exerts a gravitational pull on the oceans, creating a bulge of water on one side of the earth. There is a corresponding bulge on the other side caused by centrifugal force (created by the spinning of the Earth). The bulges are high tides and as the earth spins, different parts pass below the bulge. We have two high tides a day, know as a semi-diurnal system.

The tides do not happen at the same time every day. This is because the moon takes 28 days to orbit the earth, so the earth has to spin that bit further each day (about 40 minutes) for any given spot to arrive under the moon and get its high tide fix.

Why is that important?

Every surf break, especially in the UK which has a large tidal range (i.e. the water goes in and out quite far), will have ideal tide conditions when the waves break the best. Spot guides, such as www.wannasurf.com, will often indicate the ideal state of tide. At some breaks you won't be able to surf at a certain state of tide because of rocks, rips or other hazards.

Also, the tide can affect the size of the waves. For example, a smaller swell will often get a little bigger as the tide pushes in (often referred to as 'on the push'). Waves will often break faster and hollower (to the point of closing out – where the whole wave breaks at once and you cannot surf it) at a lower tide. At high tide, they will often be slower and backing off or not breaking properly. Learn your local beaches' best options to be one step ahead!

What is a spring tide?

Tides move from 'springs' to 'neaps' (and not just in spring). The tidal range is at its greatest on a spring tide. Spring tides happen just after the full and new moon and neaps happen at half moon. Here, the sun exerts its influence. If the sun and moon are in line (one either side or both on one side of the earth) the gravitational pull is larger and the bulges are larger – this is a spring tide. If the sun and moon are pulling in opposition, you get neaps. The differences in height and the speed at which the tides move (faster on springs) can make a difference to your break. Don't worry about it too much at first though!

More tools for swell forecasting

- Tide tables – buy a tide table for a pound or two or go online to http://easytide.ukho.gov.uk, which uses the official UK Hydrographic Office data. Remember to check if your table adjusts for British Summer Time or not.

- Applications – good iPhone apps include Magicseaweed, XCweather, Buoy Data, WindGuru and Day Tides. Surf Watch will send you alerts when your pre-set preferred conditions are forecast.

- TV forecasts – less useful than websites these days, remember to look out for a nice, fat, low pressure moving our way.

- Spot guides – www.wannasurf.com or any of the excellent UK surf guidebooks will tell you which winds, swell directions and so on are idea for UK beaches.

Types of waves

Once the swell has been generated, watched by thousands of eager eyes, what it looks like when it makes landfall is now of paramount importance. Waves come in all shapes and sizes and break on different types of beaches and reefs. The shape of the ocean floor is called its 'bathymetry'.

Parts of the wave

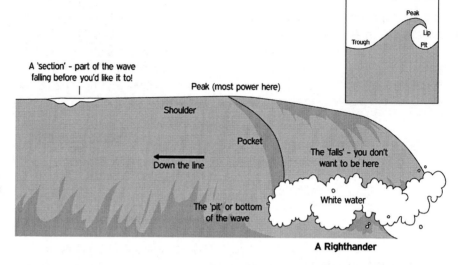

A 'section' - part of the wave falling before you'd like it to!

Peak (most power here)

Shoulder

Pocket

Down the line

The 'falls' - you don't want to be here

The 'pit' or bottom of the wave

White water

A Righthander

Peak

Trough

Lip

Pit

'As a beginner, you will start off surfing the white water, which is the line of water that tumbles shorewards once the wave has broken.'

As a beginner, you will start off surfing the white water, which is the line of water that tumbles shorewards once the wave has broken. As a rule, it doesn't really matter at this stage whether the waves 'out the back' (the unbroken peelers that more experienced surfers ride) are 1ft or 10ft. By the time they roll into waist-depth water, they should have something to offer you. This kind of wave will pick up a longboard or swell board and allow you to get to your feet before the power disappears. What a white water wave won't easily do is pick up a shortboard, so make sure that you have a board with plenty of volume.

- Crumbling – waves in the UK are often fairly weak and will crumble from top to bottom, breaking relatively slowly and providing a not-too-steep wave face to ride on. These are good for beginners as the power won't overwhelm you.

- Sectioning – a wave that breaks in several places along its length at once. These give shorter rides, but more opportunities if you're in a crowd.

- Peeling wave – a wave that breaks uniformly from the peak all the way along in one motion from left to right or vice versa.

- Pitching wave – a fast-breaking wave for good surfers.

- Barrels – a wave that pitches out far enough will create the surfer's ultimate wave, a barrel or tube. Surfers with enough skill can hitch a ride inside the curl of the wave, racing the lip as it throws out in front of them.

- Lefthander – a wave that breaks from left to right when seen from the beach. The surfer is riding to their left.

- Righthander – a wave that breaks from right to left when seen from the beach. The surfer rides to their right.

- A-frame – a wave that peaks up and breaks giving both a lefthander and righthander at the same time.

- Closeout – a wave that breaks all at once; also termed a straighthander because all you can do is ride straight in towards the shore. Closeouts are bad!

Types of breaks

A 'break' is surfer-speak for a beach which has rideable waves, i.e. waves that break. There are a few different types; the UK has loads of beach breaks but also some quality point and reef breaks.

- Beach break – sandy-bottomed beaches, ideal for learning on. How the waves break depends on the formation of the sand underneath – can be great, can be awful and often changes!

- Point break – when a swell hits a projection of solid ground, be it a manmade groyne (the fences that prevent erosion of beaches), pier or breakwater or a natural headland, a wave will break where its energy meets the land, then peel off. Pointbreaks can provide very long rides, and also very long paddles as the currents tend to be stronger. Take care as a beginner – ask for local advice.

- Reef break – rock, coral or other hardness beneath the waves. Reefbreaks usually create better shaped waves that break more predictably than beach breaks, but they are also more dangerous, break faster and will have a pack of hungry, skilled surfers on them. Do not attempt as a beginner.

Rips and currents, which affect the waves and definitely affect your surfing safety, are covered in the next chapter.

'A "break" is surfer-speak for a beach which has rideable waves, i.e. waves that break. There are a few different types; the UK has loads of beach breaks but also some quality point and reef breaks.'

Summing Up

- Suss out your nearest break, or the one you are planning to ride next, is it a point, reef or beach break? What is the optimum state of tide? What's the best wind (remember, it doesn't have to be offshore to be rideable)? Are there any dangers you need to know about?

- If you can get to the beach or see a good webcam, spend five minutes identifying types of waves – crumbling, sectioning, peeling, maybe even barrelling if you're lucky!

- Get yourself a tide table, or bookmark the right page on the UKHO website.

- Borrow or buy a surf spot guidebook such as the *Footprint Guide to Surfing in Britain*.

- Get on the computer and check out the websites listed in this chapter and any others you can find for webcams etc.

- Get into the habit of firing up all your bookmarked web pages every morning, to get a quick forecast. This will save you missing any good swells!

Chapter Three

Surf Safety and Rules

Surfing doesn't have many rules – it's a casual, fun sport with a laid-back image, after all – but there is plenty of safety stuff you need to know before you head out there. If you take a lesson with a Surfing GB qualified instructor, you'll learn all of this out there on the beach, which is ideal. But if you learn nothing else, learn the drop in rule!

Drop in rule

This is the golden rule: the surfer closest to the peak has right of way. That means you don't take off further along the wave, and it also means that you must paddle to get out of their way if you are inside of them. To clarify, the peak is the most powerful part of the wave, where it is just beginning to break (see below).

'The surfer closest to the peak has right of way. That means you don't take off further along the wave, and it also means that you must paddle to get out of their way if you are inside of them.'

Has right of way

Peak

Don't even think about it!

Snaking

If you are sitting in pole position for a wave, or paddling for one, and someone sneaks past you to get into the prime spot, they have snaked you. This is bad manners. It's often best to let this go, but if they are repeat offenders or put you or anyone else in danger by this hassling, let them know about it (nicely, of course!). A bit of 'stink-eye' (a dirty look) will often do the trick. Some surfers will conclude that constant snaking means they have every right to drop in (see above) on the offender, but this is a dangerous practice.

'When you first start surfing, it's quite daunting to take a large, unwieldy object into the sea and have it thrown around by the waves. That's why you have to paddle out safely.'

Paddling out

When you first start surfing, it's quite daunting to take a large, unwieldy object into the sea and have it thrown around by the waves. That's why you have to paddle out safely. Chapter 4 covers how to paddle out in detail, but the main safety points are below:

- Put your leash on at the water's edge. Make sure it's secure and that the swivel (the metal attachment between leash cuff and the cord at your ankle) is sticking out on the outside of your ankle so it's not in the way.

- Hold your board to one side of you. Never, ever have your board side on to the incoming waves.

- Try to paddle out with plenty of space around you, and never behind someone else. Also, don't paddle out where you will be in the way of the best part of the breaking waves as you reach the lineup.

- Paddle out of the way of surfers who are up and riding, even if this means you will take a beating in the white water!

Falling off

Otherwise known as wiping out, this is the bit that looks painful and scary, and it can be. Chapter 4 covers how to wipe out as safely as possible. You need to stay aware of your board's whereabouts as much as possible.

Surfing in crowds

This will happen to you! UK and worldwide, surfing has exploded in popularity and getting a break all to yourself is a rare pleasure. You will need to learn how to manoeuvre yourself around all sorts of craft and lots of people who may not know or care about basic safety in the water. In essence, you need to keep your eyes and ears open.

Hassling and a bad atmosphere in the water is an unfortunate occurrence. Localism is the term given to aggro given by local surfers to others on 'their' break. Some breaks are worse than others, but in the UK hassling and localism are not generally much of a problem. It's worth paddling to another section of the beach or even just getting out – surfing is supposed to be fun, so if you find yourself getting tense and angry, you're going to have a bad surf no matter what.

Avoid all forms of kayak, they are lethal in the surf. Paddle to another peak if you have to. Stand-up paddleboards are a similar danger, unless being surfed by the very best of waterman (or woman).

Bodyboarders surf smaller and softer boards, but they are also a lot faster and often unpredictable – they can spin into a takeoff a lot faster than most surfers. The more you surf with them, the more you will learn what they are likely to do.

'You will need to learn how to manoeuvre yourself around all sorts of craft and lots of people who may not know or care about basic safety in the water.'

Rips and currents

What exactly is a rip and why is it there?

Waves break with varying degrees of force along the beach, and this pattern of weak and strong flow creates sections of water moving inshore then back out. Waves break along the beach at the shallowest point, usually a sandbar. The water that has come in to shore then finds the easiest way back out, usually in a deeper channel of water next to the sandbar. This is a rip – a flow of water moving out from the beach.

Current or longshore drift is what will sweep you sideways (but many people also call these rips). Rips often form in breaks between sandbanks and near piers, groynes and so on. Depending on the beach and conditions, rips can appear in seconds or they can always be in pretty much the same place.

Rips can be hard to identify; under most tide and swell conditions they are likely to be fairly slow and won't cause you too many problems, so there's no need to worry. Lifeguards watch out for sandbanks they think are likely to collapse and start a sudden rip current. This type of rip can be very dangerous, sweeping people out into deeper, colder water very fast and causing panic. Generally, the bigger the surf, the stronger the currents, so use your common sense and powers of observation, and listen to the lifeguards' advice.

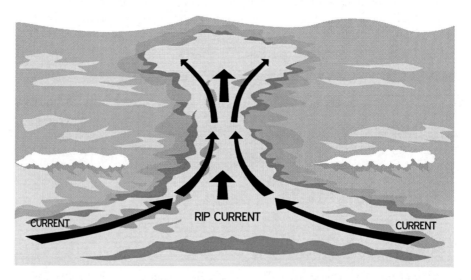

How to identify a rip

Sit and check out the surf before you go in – this will help make your whole surf session more enjoyable, as you can decide which bank/peak/area to surf, work out how many waves break in a set and how long the lulls are. Most important, of course, you can check where the rips and currents are. Look for darker water, suspended sand, and choppy mini-wavelets on top of the water from the pull of the rip. The waves might not be breaking at all in the rip, or at least not properly. There might be some foam, seaweed or debris moving steadily out to sea.

Handling rips

Once you've identified the rips, you can either avoid them completely or use them to your advantage. A rip will often develop next to a nice peak and provide an easy route to the takeoff spot for experienced surfers. You need to know where the rip is, which often means having local knowledge. Don't use a rip to get out back if it is very strong, you are not sure where it finishes or if you are not a strong paddler.

Once you've got yourself out back, sit up and take a few breaths! Then turn and line up two markers on the shore, so you'll know if you're drifting in a longshore current, which can prove as dangerous as a rip.

What to do if you get into trouble:

- If you get stuck in a rip don't leave your board, it's your life preserver.

- Don't try to paddle directly against a rip. Paddle horizontal to the beach (rips are often only 10-20m wide) or ride it out, paddle in and come in on the white water.

- The universal signal to attract help is waving one arm slowly above your head.

- The main thing is not to panic. If you have been sensible and are not surfing conditions far out of your league, you can and will get yourself out of the situation.

Surf schools

It's one of those things that people who've been on a board since age six sometimes sneer at, but those who've been to a good surf school will tell you it's an invaluable experience – and loads of fun. There are so many advantages: equipment hire included, learning water safety, have fun with other learners, tips on how to read the weather and predict swells and more. Surfing GB-approved schools will teach to proven standards and all their instructors have a lifeguard qualification.

Surf schools are a safe, fun way to get onto your feet and really surfing in the shortest time possible. Many people will stand up and ride a wave for a few seconds on their first try, and this is because they have learned the proper technique and have been given the confidence they need. If you possibly can, take at least one lesson, and if you want to really nail it, spend a week at a good Surfing GB-approved school.

Surfing GB is the governing body for the sport in the UK and they maintain a list of schools here and abroad who have to stick to certain standards and whose instructors have all undergone training with them. Surfing GB Level 1 is the basic instructor standard and perfect for beginners; if you want more tuition then look for more experienced coaches with Level 2 and upwards.

Surf schools will lend you equipment, and you will usually learn on a swell board. These blue and yellow monsters are big, soft and easy to get to your feet on. They don't look very cool, but they work! Many good surfers enjoy taking them out on smaller days to have fun with, so don't be embarrassed by using one. You can also hire them from many beaches, so you can continue to practise after you are done with lessons.

Many surf schools will offer additional services – some will make your life easier, like accommodation and food, others will really help with your surfing, like videoing you and taking photos. Check out the Surfing GB website to find a school in a convenient location for you. You really can knock months off your learning time with a good surf school, so check out the ones in your area.

Sun sense

Slip, slop and slap – even on fairly cloudy days, the sun can still do you damage and skin cancer is on the rise. Always wear a water resistant, high-factor sunscreen when surfing. You can be in the water for several hours, and the sun reflecting off the water will burn you even faster than usual. If you're

'Always wear a water resistant, high-factor sunscreen when surfing. You can be in the water for several hours, and the sun reflecting off the water will burn you even faster than usual.'

surfing somewhere hot, you can get rash vests that protect from UV rays. Take care on sunny days where the temperature is lower because of a breeze – it might feel colder, but the sun will still catch you.

Out of the water, cover up when you've had enough sun and wear good sunglasses to protect your eyes. A hat will protect your head when the sun is strong. Make sure you drink plenty to avoid dehydration, and seek shade during the middle of the day when it's really sunny.

Pollution and critters

Scary creatures and water pollution – the things you don't want in the water with you! Surfers Against Sewage (SAS) are the UK charity who look after our interests and have done loads to clean up the beaches, but the fight goes on, especially against marine litter, storm drain overflows and oil spills at sea. If you get ill after being in the water, report it to them as they maintain a database to help with their campaigns. It's not as much of a worry as it used to be, but ear and throat infections and stomach upsets have happened to most surfers.

Joining SAS is worthwhile, and you can take part in litter picks, social events like the famous SAS Ball and other campaign events. All surfers should be aware of the precious natural resources of the coastal areas and the ocean itself and what they can do to help – it's your duty.

As for marine life, there's very little to threaten you in UK waters – you might see a basking shark but they won't hurt you, and if you do see a fin it's only going to be a friendly dolphin. Seals are no trouble as long as you stay away from their colonies – sometimes they get curious and come to have a look at surfers. It's wonderful when they come close and play, but don't touch as they can bite! Weever fish and jellyfish are your main worries.

Weever fish have sharp spines and skulk around on the sandy bottom of the sea. If you get spiked, immerse your foot in hot (as hot as you can stand, but not scalding) water. For jellyfish stings, do not rub them as this will intensify the pain. Spray the area with sea water and apply ice or a cold compress if available. Lifeguards are used to treating these injuries, so ask for their help.

'Weever fish have sharp spines and skulk around on the sandy bottom of the sea. If you get spiked, immerse your foot in hot (as hot as you can stand, but not scalding) water.'

What you can do to protect the surfing environment:

- Dispose of rubbish wisely – chewing gum and cigarette butts take 10 years to biodegrade, so even the smallest bits of rubbish can pollute for a long time!

- Reduce, reuse and recycle, in that order – most councils now recycle, so make the most of it.

- Use natural alternatives to harsh cleaning products, fertilisers and other chemicals where possible.

- Take a look at bamboo wetsuits, eco-friendly boards and wax – these things are in development and need surfers' support.

- Bag it, bin it – don't flush it. Non-biodegradables and things like panty liners shouldn't go down the toilet. They end up in storm drains and can get onto the beach, yuk!

- Get involved – report pollution incidences and join SAS. Have your voice heard.

- Pick it up – get in the habit of picking up one piece of litter at the beach every time you head back after a surf. Yes, you shouldn't have to clean up other people's mess, but it might save the life of a marine creature, so it's worth your time.

First aid and emergencies

Surfing isn't a sport that's likely to injure you too badly, but accidents do happen, so it's best to be aware of basic first aid and where to get help. When you get to the beach, check out the facilities it has – are there lifeguards around, or is there an emergency phone or at least a rescue buoy? Dial 999 or 112 and ask for the coastguard if you or anyone else gets into trouble.

If you are driving to the beach you should have a basic first aid kit in your car. If you want to train to be a lifeguard yourself (and the qualification is great fun as well as helpful in many situations) then get in touch with the RNLI (Royal National Lifeboat Institution) at www.rnli.org.uk.

Lifeguards and flags

The RNLI and local councils run a UK lifeguard service in the summer months at the most popular beaches around the country. Lifeguards are paid to patrol the beaches and keep them safe; they have a wealth of knowledge and understanding of the sea and are often surfers themselves. If you rock up at a new beach, it's never a bad idea to have a word with one of the lifeguards to ask where the best place to paddle out and surf is.

The lifeguards will put flags up on the beach to show people where to swim and surf. A red flag means the beach is closed, or at least a certain section is – there may be danger from a rip or submerged rocks, so take notice of this. Red and yellow flags are for the swimmers and bodyboarders (though experienced bodyboarders wearing proper fins on their feet will often surf the better peaks with the standup surfers). Don't go within this area or the lifeguards will embarrass you by using loudhailers and even jet-skis to move you over! Black and white flags are for surfing between. These are the patrolled areas of the beach; if you surf outside of these areas you are pretty much on your own.

'Black and white flags are for surfing between. These are the patrolled areas of the beach; if you surf outside of these areas you are pretty much on your own.'

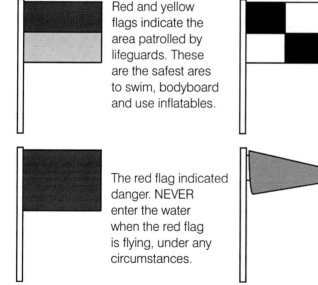

Red and yellow flags indicate the area patrolled by lifeguards. These are the safest ares to swim, bodyboard and use inflatables.

Black and white chequered flags indicate an area zoned by lifeguards for use of watercraft such as surfboards and kayaks. Never swim or bodyboard in these areas.

The red flag indicated danger. NEVER enter the water when the red flag is flying, under any circumstances.

The orange windsock indicates offshore wind conditions. You should NEVER use an inflatable when the sock is flying.

If the lifeguards ask you to do something, they are asking for a reason, and it is in your interest and the interest of everyone's safety that you do as requested. If, for example, you are surfing outside of the flags, they may ask you to move between them so they can keep an eye on you. Just because there may be other surfers outside of the flags doesn't mean you should be!

A healthy respect for the ocean and its power, a dollop of common sense and taking note of these few rules will keep you safe and happy in the surf. Ocean knowledge is something a bit different, and it cannot be learned just by reading books. There is just no substitute for getting out there on the beach and among the waves, catching, learning and practising. The more different kinds of situations and surf conditions you experience, the faster and deeper your ocean knowledge will become. Even the oldest and most experienced waterman or woman is still learning, and can still be surprised by the sea. Take care, and enjoy the experience!

'There is just no substitute for getting out there on the beach and among the waves, catching, learning and practising.'

Summing Up

■ Next time you're at the beach, really take a look around to see what emergency equipment and signs are around.

■ Sit up high on the dunes (if possible) and try to identify the rips and currents running on the beach. Ask the lifeguards to see if you've got it right!

■ Check out www.surfinggb.com to see where your nearest approved surf school is.

■ Check out www.sas.org.uk to see how you can help.

■ Check out www.rnli.org.uk for the latest and best safety information for all water users.

Chapter Four

First Steps

There's a hell of a lot to remember when you first start surfing, and you won't get it right first time or every time. Relax and enjoy it – even the best surfers make idiots of themselves with the basics at times! After a few sessions it will all come together and you'll be able to start using more of the tips given here in order to progress your surfing.

Which foot?

You are either a natural or goofy-footed surfer – left foot forward is natural, right foot forward is goofy. A very few talented people can ride switch-foot with either foot in front. To work out which you are, think of your stance on a snowboard or skateboard, or do a dry-land pop-up and see which feels most natural. It's always possible that you may be natural surfing but goofy snowboarding, but don't worry if this is the case, go with whatever feels the most natural. Your leash goes on the back foot and secures snug around the ankle. Now paddle out, and you're ready, finally, to stand up and be counted as a surfer!

Walking down

Now, it might seem mad to give you instructions on how to walk to the water's edge, but it's better to be safe than sorry, and falling over before you've even got wet is not a good look!

Once you're suited up, tuck your board under your arm nose first, fins in – this isn't set in stone, but it means you have control of the sharpest bits of the board and so are less likely to hurt anyone. Your leash is either wrapped

'There's a hell of a lot to remember when you first start surfing, and you won't get it right first time or every time.'

around the tail and fins of the board (loosely, so you don't damage it) or coiled loosely and held in the same hand your board is in. Don't let it drag in the sand – looks uncool and shortens its life. If it's windy, hold on tight!

Walk down the beach, checking out the waves as you go but watch out for trip hazards like big stones or little kids! Stop a few metres before you get to where the waves are lapping up and put your board down, usually deck upwards so that it's less likely to blow away – you can also push the tail gently into the sand to anchor the fins. Do any warming up you need to. The put the leash around the ankle of your back foot (under or on top of your wetsuit, whichever suits you) and fasten the Velcro securely. Pick up your board and begin to wade out with it held on one side of you facing straight out to sea.

'As a beginner, paddling out means wading into about chest deep water, then turning the board and surfing the already broken white water waves.'

Surfing the white water

Paddling out is the term given to entering the water, wading out, lying on the board and paddling past the line of the breaking waves to the relative safety that lies beyond. As a beginner, paddling out means wading into about chest deep water, then turning the board and surfing the already broken white water waves.

- Pick a wave that has broken and has been rolling towards you for a second or two. If it has broken a split second beforehand, the energy will be too explosive unless it really is a tiny wave.

- Point the nose of the board straight to the shore.

- Lie on your board well before the line of water hits.

- Dig one arm deep into the water at the side of the board and propel yourself forward. Use alternate strokes.

- Keep your head, shoulders and chest off the board as you paddle, and keep your legs together.

- When the white water hits you, paddle for a couple more strokes and let the board stabilise a bit.

- Pop up (see opposite).

Take off – popping up

- When the wave has got you and the board is moving forward, pop up onto your feet in one smooth movement: both hands go flat on the deck of the board and you push your chest off, followed by the rest of your torso.

- Then jump and shove your front foot under you.

- Your back foot will follow and should land near the tail, ideally between the fins.

- Stay low to keep your balance, knees bent and arms out to avoid wobbles.

- Don't stick your bum out or you'll surf with the dreaded 'poo-man' stance.

- Most of your weight should be on your back foot. To help with this, try to keep the back knee more bent than the front.

- You can use one knee to pop up, but this is a bad habit you should try to avoid getting into! You need to be up fast so the power of the wave stays with you.

- Your front arm needs to be straight out, slightly bent and leading over the nose of the board.

- Your back arm needs to be at about a 90 degree angle, with your hand in front of you just above your waist.

'Pop up onto your feet in one smooth movement: both hands go flat on the deck of the board and you push your chest off, followed by the rest of your torso.'

Green waves

When you are bored with white water waves and are standing up two out of three times and riding them in, you're ready to try small green waves, and you need to be able to paddle out to them. Don't worry too much at first about how big is too big – in general, if you can't paddle out there, you shouldn't be there, so if you can make it out, you should be all right. Use your common sense here.

- Wade out to about chest deep water.

- Wait for a lull in the waves.

- Jump onto the board (lying down).

- Balance yourself – the nose of the board should be out of the water, but not by much. Don't sink the tail too far or you'll find it super-hard to move forward. Knowledge of positioning only comes with practise.

'When you are bored with white water waves and are standing up two out of three times and riding them in, you're ready to try small green waves.'

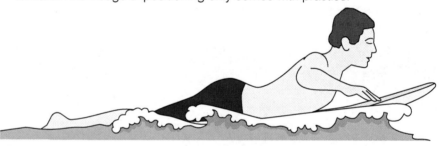

- Dig alternate arms into the water as deep as you can, stretching forward as far as you can. Many surfers use an s-shaped stroke under the water, like with front crawl. Hands are loosely cupped.

- Keep your chest up and back arched. It feels odd but works best, and you can see where you're going.

- Legs together, or you'll look like a kook.

- If you're riding a big board, avoid breaking and broken waves by rolling your board and yourself over. The wave will pass over and you can roll back up. This is known as a turtle roll, see opposite.

- For smaller boards, learn to duck-dive – see page 48. Duck-diving isn't easy, so at first, paddle as hard as you can towards the wave, push yourself up off the board and let the wave or white water rush between you and the board. The downside of this is you will get pushed backwards and have to make up the distance again.

- If you want to bail your board (and you really, really shouldn't) then check around you for other surfers, then slide off and dive under the wave. Grab your leash and pull the board back to you, then wriggle on it and start over again. Bailing wastes time and energy, and loose boards are dangerous, so try to avoid this.

- Keep paddling and duck-diving until you reach the lineup where all the other surfers are, or where the waves pass you by without breaking.

- Now check the shore and line yourself up with two points. Keep checking this as you surf to make sure you are not drifting all over the place.

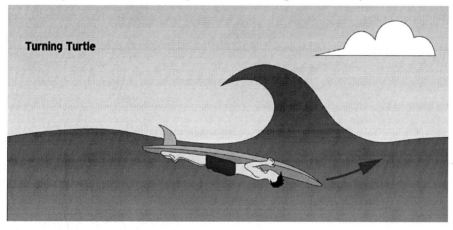

Turning Turtle

Choose your wave and paddle for it

- Keep looking out to sea. Sounds obvious, but people are caught unawares chatting/daydreaming all the time!

- Wait for a set to appear – lines of water humping up on the horizon. If nothing else alerts you to this, other surfers' excitement and movement will!

- Choose a wave that looks like it will break close to you, or that you think you can get into position for, and one that doesn't have tons of other people going for it.

- Turn your board, lie down on it and paddle, either straight into shore or along a bit so you can get into the best position.

- You want to be a touch further forward on your board than you are when paddling out; this way you will catch the waves easier. Arch your back a bit more.

- As the wave approaches, paddle hard to gain speed. You have to really want the wave or you will miss it, so don't be half-hearted.

- You can angle your board in the direction you are going or straight ahead.

- As you feel the wave lift you, paddle until the board is moving and you feel that you have caught the wave.

- Put in two extra paddle strokes to make sure.

- Check left and right to make sure you are not going to drop in on anyone. Most important! See page 29.

- Pop up!

Don't miss out – tips

- If the wave you've gone for passes underneath you it either means you have started to paddle for it too late, or you are too far back on your board.

- If the wave breaks on top of you, you have started paddling for it too close to the shore and need to move out a bit further.

- If you catch the wave, but stand up and it drops you off the back, you have missed out those extra two or three paddle strokes and not quite caught the wave. Frustrating!

- One common beginner's mistake is to be too far out. You need to be where the energy is, scary though this can be, you need to get amongst it.

Paddling for waves – tips

If you're too far back on the board and the tail is sunk too far, you will never catch a wave – they will all pass you by. If you are too far forward, the nose will dig into the water and you will be thrown off forward by the wave; this is also known as 'pearling' and isn't much fun! You should practise paddling in calm water so that you can find the balance on the board, and also try sitting up on it (a skill which is harder than it sounds, and which you will need once you are paddling out beyond the white water).

When paddling, keep your chest up off the board, your back arched, and paddle with deep strokes. It means you can see what's going on, you'll catch waves easier and paddle faster (even though the position feels strange at first; watch other surfers, they all do it) and once you've caught the wave and try to stand, your chest is already off the board so you're not having to push so much of your weight so far up with your arms.

Trimming

Once you're up and riding, keeping the board in trim involves shifting your weight as the wave moves to keep your balance and keep the board moving sideways along the wave. This is a matter of instinct, so practise will make perfect. Lean backwards, and the nose of the board will come up, lean forwards and you will speed up and the nose will dip down. The board moves smoothly and converts the wave's power into speed when you are properly in trim.

Duck-diving

When you get onto a shorter board and are paddling out past the lines of white water to tackle green unbroken waves, you'll need to be able to duck-dive. This is a hard thing to learn, but persevere.

- Time your paddle out for a break in the waves and choose a spot where a rip can help you get out or where the waves aren't breaking as much.

- Paddle hard towards the oncoming wave.

- About 2ft before the wave reaches you, grab the rails of your board halfway between the middle and the nose and push down, sinking the nose of your board under the water.

- Keep your arms straight, point your head down and let your body follow. Make sure you have taken a nice deep breath.

- As the wave goes over you, put your knee or foot onto the deck of the board and push it down and deeper. Your other leg trails out behind you.

- Let your buoyancy pop you back towards the surface. You can pull on the board as well if you like – take care not to smack yourself in the face though!

- Start to paddle again, and get ready for the next one!

'When you get onto a shorter board and are paddling out past the lines of white water to tackle green unbroken waves, you'll need to be able to duck-dive.'

Duckdiving

Wiping out

How to fall off safely and recover as fast as you can is a skill well worth learning! This one comes with experience, but here are a few points to note. Wiping out is an intrinsic part of surfing, and you might as well roll with the punches. It's the ocean's karma – sometimes you get some good ones, sometimes you get a flogging.

Firstly, the fear of wiping out is natural, but you have to learn to deal with it. Most wipeouts last just five or 10 seconds, unless you're into some big, powerful waves! Most people can hold their breath easily in a pool for about 30 seconds. The problem is that you don't think you can last out when you're being thrown around by a wave. You're underwater, you can't see or hear anything and the violence of all that water around you (and the suddenly lethal weapon that is your board) is disorientating and scary.

There's one thing you really need to do, and it isn't easy: let go and realise you just can't fight it. Relax and you will come up.

If you're on a white water wave, there's not much power left in it as it's already broken, so plop off away from your board and wait until you come up. If you're on a smallish green wave, you might well be heading for the bottom! Don't dive if it's shallow. Otherwise, try to dive through the back of the wave or as deep as you can to avoid the worst of the breaking wave's power. If it's small enough you might be able to jump over the back. If it's bigger, there's not a lot you can do but let it happen.

You might have some forewarning that you're coming off and be able to jump away from your board or push it away with your legs. Never do this if your board might injure someone else in the water and never dive off head first in shallow water. Be aware that there may be rocks or other hazards around. When you surface, use your arms to protect your head.

Alternatively, you might just have a split second of realisation before you're hurled into the pit. In this case all you can do before you hit the water is take a deep breath and try to notice what's happening around you. Having some idea of how many waves are behind you in the set, how far away the next one is, where other people are and where your board is will help once you come

'How to fall off safely and recover as fast as you can is a skill well worth learning!'

up. While you're down, though, just relax again. There's not much else you can do. With more experience, you'll find the ways that suit you and your board for staying out of trouble.

Don't panic. You'll use up your oxygen faster, and it won't get you anywhere. You will be frightened plenty of times when you surf, but you have to learn that you can't be in total control of the situation. The fear sets your adrenaline going, and this is a good thing. It sharpens your perceptions and instincts and lets you get out of those situations you most dread.

There are things you can do to help you deal with wipe outs. Firstly, get out there. Swim, surf, bodysurf, bodyboard and experience the power of waves and learn about how they break at every opportunity. Get used to the power of the ocean. Watch other people and how they fall off different boards and different waves. Fitness is also important – when you're tired, you struggle more to catch your breath and get back on the board. So you need to increase your cardiovascular fitness – swimming and paddling practise are ideal. Yoga helps with controlling your breathing and staying calm and focused.

Summing Up

■ Practise popping up on dry land. Jump up and check your stance, then do it again about 10 times. It needs to be an automatic reaction, as you don't have a lot of time to get it right out there in the sea.

■ Watch some surf films and identify the basic moves. Watch how the bottom turn sets up everything a surfer does. Check out their body positioning and how they use their arms.

■ Do some swim training and see how far you can swim underwater holding your breath. This will help with confidence during wipeouts.

■ Find a yoga class or do a taster session to improve your breathing.

■ Practise your paddling even when it's flat – great for fitness too.

Chapter Five

Manoeuvres

Once you're really surfing, it's time to throw some moves in there. Your starting points are bottom turns and trimming along the face of green waves, closely followed by top turns, then cutbacks. Once you are pulling these off with a certain amount of confidence, you can call yourself an intermediate surfer.

Then you will move on to re-entries, floaters, off-the-lips, airs, barrels … that's a bit beyond the scope of this book, but we'll take a look anyway, so you know what you're looking at when you see others doing them.

Bottom turns

The first manoeuvre every surfer learns is a bottom turn. At first you will already be at the bottom of the wave, since it's just a line of white water, but once on green waves you will surf from the top to the bottom and then need to turn to carry on along the face of the wave. The bottom turn is essential, a solid one is required to set up any other moves you want to do.

- At the bottom of the wave, lean onto the inside rail. Pressure on your back foot keeps the fins and back of the board in the wave and helps the turn.

- If your board stalls or digs into the wave face (digs a rail) and throws you off, you have put too much weight on the tail or rail. If it doesn't turn, you haven't put enough pressure on. Only experience will tell you how much pressure to apply, and it changes for different waves.

- Keep your legs bent, storing energy.

- Keep your shoulders open and point with your front arm where you want to go – this ensures your shoulders are heading the right way! Look where you want to go – never down at the board.

'The first manoeuvre every surfer learns is a bottom turn.'

- Allow the board to keep turning, straightening your legs and using their power to keep moving. Until you are heading where you want to go – either up the wave face in order to do a top turn (or other manoeuvre) or along the wave so you can trim along the face.

This describes a forehand bottom turn, where you are facing the wave as you turn. If you are surfing backhand with your back to the wave, it's a bit different as you need to lean backwards to put pressure on the outside rail. Otherwise, use your shoulders, arms and bent knees in the same way to bring you around smoothly. Remember to look and point to turn, and everything else will follow. Don't avoid going backhand, or you'll be avoiding half the waves and breaks out there!

Need2Know

Top turns

A top turn is a turn executed at the top or lip of the wave and is sometimes called an off-the-lip. The top turn naturally follows the bottom turn, as your bottom turn has sent the board towards the lip.

- Coming out of the bottom turn, guide your board ahead towards the lip. Look where you want to go.

- As you get to the lip, put your weight on your back foot and use your front foot to guide the board round.

- Keep turning until you are heading back down the face of the wave.

As you first start to link turns, it's fine to turn in smaller arcs or 'S' turns – as you get better, your turns will get more powerful and vertical – confidence and power is the key. Study videos and pictures of surfers to get the idea.

Cutbacks

Linking turns and trimming along the wave face will eventually mean you run too far ahead of the power. This is when you need to do a cutback, essentially a top turn followed by a bottom turn in quick succession to put you back into the pocket (right by the peak where the power of the wave is).

■ You'll know when you need to do a cutback – the board will be losing speed and the wave becomes too flat.

■ Head up towards the top of the wave and do a top turn.

■ Open your shoulders and point backwards in the direction you want to go – i.e. towards the pocket.

■ Put your weight on your back foot and guide the board around. Keep low here.

■ Now you need to bottom turn before you hit the white water. Timing is important here so that you have enough power and momentum to get around without stalling the board (a common problem with cutting back, especially when the waves are weak).

■ Pivot on your back foot with most of your weight over the tail of the board, turning the board much as you would for a bottom turn.

■ Extend out of the turn, using the power in your legs and redirect it back down the line.

■ Don't try to force it or hurry it too much, let the energy of the wave work for you.

'You'll know when you need to do a cutback – the board will be losing speed and the wave becomes too flat.'

Need2Know

Re-entries

Heading down the wave and seeing it section (break prematurely) in front of you can be disheartening, but not if you can whack a re-entry off it.

- Power towards that ball of white water.

- Do a nice bottom turn and head for the top of the wave where it's beginning to break in front of you.

- Top turn as hard as you can.

- Absorb the impact with your knees and pull the board around so that you come down with the white water. Lean back to avoid pearling.

- Ride out.

Floaters

A floater is used to float you over a section that has broken and get you back onto the green face.

- Do a bottom turn.

- Head towards the lip as fast as you can.

- Steer your board along the top of the lip, staying low and keeping your arms wide for balance.

- Allow the board to drop down, hopefully onto green wave face, or into the trough in front of the white water, and continue.

Need2Know

Snaps

A snap is basically a more radical top turn.

- Pull a good solid bottom turn.

- Aim for the lip, getting as vertical as possible.

- When the nose of the board is projecting out of the lip, lean hard on your back foot and twist your head and shoulders, guiding the board with your front foot. Commit to it and go as hard as you can for maximum spray!

- Remember to use your arms to keep your balance, keep your shoulders open and point and look where you want to go.

Advanced moves

Some of the other stuff you might see being pulled off by surfers who rip are:

Tailslide

A tailslide is a top turn where the fins are released at the top (aided by a good shove with the back foot) and the board slides around. This takes practice and a great amount of control. Slide that tail far enough, and you'll pull a 360!

Tubes

'Riding the barrel is seen as the pinnacle of surfing prowess and the best surfing experience there is by many surfers. It is not easy!'

Riding the barrel is seen as the pinnacle of surfing prowess and the best surfing experience there is by many surfers. It is not easy! There isn't an over-abundance of barrelling waves in the UK, so although it is perfectly possible to get barrelled here if that's what you're trying to learn, you're better off taking a trip somewhere like Indonesia where there are barrels galore. Barrelling waves are always steep and powerful, and as such are only for advanced surfers.

Airs

The first air anyone does is a chop-hop – barely leaving the water, just kicking out the nose then fins and landing again. It's done on any section that will provide a little ramp to gain some speed on.

Watch any of the new-school surfers like Dane Reynolds, Ry Craike, Jordy Smith and so on to see all of the moves mentioned in this chapter and more put together in crazy combos that you won't believe they can ride out of. This is new-school surfing at its best.

Bigger waves

Wave riding is all about confidence – when you first start surfing, anything over 1-2ft can look a bit scary! As you learn more about the ocean and grow in skill, you will naturally want to ride larger waves for the thrill and power they offer. Make sure you can handle the conditions – feeling a bit apprehensive is fine, as you should never underestimate the ocean, but charging out into conditions that you can't handle can be really dangerous.

■ Know your limits – don't surf waves way bigger than anything you've surfed before.

■ But, you should also push yourself – you might well be surprised what you can achieve!

■ Be prepared – make sure all your equipment is in order and that you are fed and rested properly.

■ Take some time to check out the conditions – be sure you know how big the sets are, when the outside sets appear, how long the lulls are, where's best to paddle out and so on. Don't just run into the water.

■ Take a mate, preferably someone who is more experienced and can bolster your confidence – in the end, you're pretty much on your own, but someone to help you choose which wave to go for can be great.

■ Catch one! Just go for a wave as soon as you are out there – or you can easily sit and psyche yourself out, getting cold and frustrated. Just do it.

'Just go for a wave as soon as you are out there – or you can easily sit and psyche yourself out, getting cold and frustrated. Just do it.'

- Don't hesitate – if you are paddling for a wave, paddle for it or don't bother, because hesitation mucks up your timing and can leave you with a set landing on your head after a nice heavy wipeout.

- Enjoy the rush of adrenaline, controlling your fear and using it to your advantage – the feeling of accomplishment when you catch a wave on a bigger day is second to none.

- Take your poundings – paddling out and duck-diving bigger sets is exhausting and you will wonder how much more you can take. Breathe, keep going and relax into the wipeouts – if you struggle you will only waste energy and precious oxygen.

Surfing really big waves, that is anything over 6ft, requires a lot of skill, fitness and experience, and especially confidence. For this, there's nothing to beat getting in the water as often as possible. Tow-surfing is a growing sport which involves being pulled into waves that are too big and fast to paddle into by a jet-ski – this is for the truly dedicated experts out there!

'If you are paddling for a wave, paddle for it or don't bother, because hesitation mucks up your timing and can leave you with a set landing on your head after a nice heavy wipeout.'

62

Summing Up

- Invest in some DVDs to help your surfing, there are quite a few instructional DVDs out there now. Try *110% Surfing Techniques volumes 1 and 2* (produced by UK surf instructor Martin Connolly, www.discoverysurf.com) and *Surfing Techniques With Tim Curran* (beginner and intermediate).

- Some books to help your surfing include *Taj Burrow's Book of Hot Surfing* – classic and a really good read. Taj is a top surfer who loves new-school moves as well as winning top-level contests. *The Surfer's Mind* by Richard Bennett is also a really good aid to surfing your best, focusing on how to train your body and mind.

- There are so many surfing DVDs out there – some will focus on new-school surfing, some contests, some travel and road trips, some more spiritual and cultural discoveries. You'll soon find out which type you like the best. To improve your own surfing, pick DVDs which feature surfers whose style you admire and want to emulate. A good DVD will feature top names and will make you want to get out there on the water yourself. Warning, they can make you really frustrated when there's been a bit of a long flat spell!

- YouTube has loads and loads of surfing clips from ASP events to free-surfers busting loose. Type a few surf brand names in and get the good stuff free. Also take a look at MPORA, which is dedicated to action sports.

Chapter Six

Surf Travel

Surfers are travellers, always searching for the next wave, the perfect wave. Surf travel comes in many forms, from a simple surf trip down the coast with a tent and a few friends, to a multi-stop round-the-world trip which leaves your family wondering if you'll ever come back.

Many surfers live quite a nomadic life, choosing to forgo the stability of a permanent job to work summers as bartenders, lifeguards and surf instructors and so on, then fly off in the winters to hotter, more consistent wave-riding locations.

So whether you're surfing home or away, here are some ideas of places to go and some of the very best waves that are out there in the world. It is undeniable that experiencing different conditions and locations improves your surfing, and travel, as the cliché has it, will broaden all your horizons. It doesn't have to be expensive either, so take a look and start planning!

UK

Road trips are a classic way to enjoy the variety that the UK surf scene offers. Youth hostelling, camping, caravanning and surf camps and guesthouses are also fun ways to do things. Here are a few of the best-loved destinations. Get your map out and do some research on the Internet if you want to find somewhere off the beaten track – which is well worth the effort.

Newquay, Cornwall

Dubbed 'surf city' by many, loads of pros, travellers and surfers of all abilities congregate here to surf the wide array of breaks, from the famous Fistral Beach to the Town Beaches (sheltered and smaller for those stormy days) and on to the wide and beautiful Watergate Bay. This place lives and breathes surfing, and with tons of surf shops it's a great place to check out and buy equipment. It also has a great nightlife (try the Red Lion, Belushi's, the Fistral Beach Bar and the Chy) and lots of hostels to stay in. Camping in the town is limited but the odd camper van is overlooked.

Croyde, Devon

Super-popular with weekend warriors due to its proximity to the motorway, Croyde boasts an amazing, heavy, low-tide bank which throws out barrels to the ever-increasing crowds that visit in the summer. It's also home to the Gold Coast Ocean Fest every summer. There's plenty of camping and tourist facilities. Try Woolacombe just to the north which has a very long beach where you can find yourself a peak; stay in the lovely Mortehoe campsite and visit the Red Barn pub. Saunton to the south, offers ideal waves for longboarding and beginners. Check out the Surfing Croyde Bay surf school which has friendly and experienced instructors.

The Gower, Wales

Surfing in Wales is centred on the south coast, with the Gower being the jewel in the crown. It's a magnet for southwesterly swell and has absolutely breathtaking unspoilt scenery. Llangennith beach, facing west at the tip of the peninsula, is one of the most consistent beach breaks. Almost three miles of sand means there are plenty of peaks to choose from at all stages of the tide. Camp at the Hill End campsite and make sure you visit the legendary PJ's surf shop. There are plenty of B&Bs and and campsites in the area.

You can also head into Swansea for a surf and some entertainment. Langland Bay and Caswell have excellent waves when bigger winter swells and strong southwesterly winds hit the Gower. Crowds and rips can be a problem at Langland but as long as you're polite and respect the locals everyone gets on fine. The Mumbles is famous for eating and drinking.

'Llangennith beach, facing west at the tip of the peninsula, is one of the most consistent beach breaks. Almost three miles of sand means there are plenty of peaks to choose from at all stages of the tide.'

Thurso, Scotland

The famous wave at Thurso East offers up cracking barrels beloved of the pro surfers who visit every spring for a World Qualifying Series event. The water is cold up here, but the surfers are a friendly and hardy bunch. Plenty of space for all, and loads of breaks to discover. Camping is the way to go although there are guesthouses aplenty.

Bundoran, Ireland

Home to the famous Peak wave, Bundoran in northwest Ireland is a typical holidaymaker's town which has grown in popularity with surfers. There are loads of places to stay, surf and party and the surrounding scenery, with Ben Bulben as the backdrop, is spectacular. The area picks up plenty of swell. The Peak is a reef break – it gets crowded and is not for beginners, so head to Tullan beach break where there are more peaks to be found. A map and a willingness to explore is essential here. The waves can be inconsistent and local knowledge is the best way to score, so you need patience too.

For backpackers, check out Bundoran Surf Lodge or the Turf 'n Surf lodge, both in the town centre. There is a lot of self-catering accommodation to choose from, along with a number of hotels and B&Bs – log on to www. goireland.com. In town, check out Brennan's, a traditional Irish bar for your traditional pint of Guinness. The Old Bridge Bar often has good traditional Irish music sessions, and there are also a few nightclubs to be found.

Europe

Peniche, Portugal

The whole coast of Portugal from the Algarve (around Sagres is perfect) to Ericeria, Peniche (the famous Supertubes), Espinho and northwards has endless beach breaks to entertain you. Peniche is great as there are waves for all abilities; also, it's a peninsula with beaches facing in all different directions, so the wind will be blowing offshore somewhere – ideal. Head there from March to September; it can be pretty rainy in spring and because the Gulf Stream doesn't hit it, it can be colder than you'd expect. Wear a 3/2mm wetty. There are loads of surf camps with qualified instructors as well as plenty of places to camp, and looking out for bargain package deals can work out really well too.

Fuerteventura, Canary Islands

With moon-like volcanic scenery, Fuerte has loads of reef breaks for the better surfer. To ease yourself in, try Cotillo and Playa Blanca, beach breaks that pick up plenty of swell. If you're confident, The Bubble is a punchy little left and right peak that breaks over reef, one of the island's most infamous waves. Most people stay in Corralejo which has endless accommodation as well as plenty of eateries and entertainment options. A cheap package deal and a £20-a-day hire car are the best way to see everything you want – the national parks are lovely. The islands come alive in the winter with raw Atlantic groundswells. Lanzarote and Tenerife also have waves and are just a ferry ride away.

'With moon-like volcanic scenery, Fuerte has loads of reef breaks for the better surfer.'

Hossegor, France

The heavy beach break barrels of southwest France are rightly famous. Hossegor hosts one of the European World Championship Tour events every September, when the plaza around Rock Food cafe is the place to be. Endless peaks on endless beaches strewn with half-naked French chicks, plus a rocking nightlife make the area an easy choice for UK surfers, many of whom drive over via the ferry. There are waves for all abilities and usually somewhere is working well in most conditions. Head further south to Biarritz for mellow waves and glamour. You can wear boardies but take a 3/2mm wetty as well. Camp for about €10 a night; plenty of hostels up to posh hotels so take your pick.

Further afield

Taghazoute, Morocco

Morocco has become the place to be in recent winters, with its cheap living and loads of righthand point breaks. A lot of the coast is deserted and undeveloped, although this is changing. Anchor Point is the most famous wave, a reeling righthand point break in the village. There are plenty of other beaches nearby, but the place is getting a bit more crowded now. Take a look at www.surfmaroc.co.uk and www.morocsurf.com for some of the best surf camps around; accommodation is generally very cheap but can be basic. Autumn and winter are best for waves and you just need a 3/2mm wetsuit. Car hire is cheap but watch out for goats and mad drivers. It's well-worth heading north along the coast road and exploring. Make sure you visit a souk for a mad shopping experience, try the mint tea, buy a super-warm beanie and eat a couple of tagines, the national dish. As it's a Muslim country, you can't buy alcohol except in larger supermarkets.

Gold Coast, Australia

The Gold Coast and Byron Bay are great spots for the travelling surfer, but it depends what you like. Many find the Gold Coast too crowded and towny, some find Byron too commercialised and far from its hippy roots. In truth, the entire coast of Oz (until you hit the Barrier Reef) is excellent for surfing. A camper van or hostelling are ideal ways to see things. You will get further buying your own banger than spending time on one of the backpacker buses, and get to see exactly what you want, i.e. waves. There's surf all year round, sunshine and down to earth, welcoming people. Surfing is part of their culture and the beach lifestyle is almost a religion. You will love it.

Costa Rica

Costa Rica has both a Caribbean coast and a Pacific coast, both of which catch plenty of waves. December to April is their dry season, and it's also offshore, consistent and warm enough to just wear boardies. The Pacific side is probably better for beginners. Head to Tamarindo, Costa Rica's surf city, and go from there. There are plenty of surf shops and schools and you can rent a cabina from £12 a night. If it goes flat, check out some of the exotic wildlife in the national parks and see the spectacular volcanoes.

The Maldives

A chain of islands southwest of Sri Lanka in the Indian Ocean, the Maldives are boat-trip paradise. Biggest and most consistent in about March to October, but any time is good and it's boardies all year round. For hassle-free surfing, a boat trip will cost roughly £80 a day; there are some land-based surf-specific resorts as well. The reefs are shallow so take a first aid kit. Fishing, sunbathing, diving and snorkelling are amazing when you're not surfing. The Maldives are the epitome of the tropical, sun and wave-drenched trip, so if you have little time but some cash, this is a great choice and will allow you to improve your surfing exponentially.

'Wrap your board up carefully if you're getting on a plane. Get hold of some bubble wrap, cardboard, pipe insulation and duct-tape, and go mad.'

Tips for trips

- Wrap your board up carefully if you're getting on a plane. Get hold of some bubble wrap, cardboard, pipe insulation and duct-tape, and go mad. It will get chucked around, and it's better to be safe than sorry. It's also worth taking a picture of it before the trip in case you need to make an insurance claim.

- Take a ding repair kit like Solarez, great for quick fixes. Spare leashes, fins, fin keys and wax never hurt anyone either.

- Take a first aid kit adapted to where you're going and what you're doing. Tend to any open wounds straight away, however small, because warm water and humidity makes them fester.

- Protect your board, wetsuit and self from the sun wherever possible.

- Get good travel insurance which will cover you for absolutely everything from losing luggage to requiring an emergency flight home for medical reasons.

- Take insect repellant, sun cream, aftersun, a big hat, mobile phone, your debit card, a credit card for emergencies, and don't forget your tickets and passport! Make copies of important documents, scan them in and email to yourself.

- Otherwise, pack light, but include something warm for the evenings.

- Check what jabs you need well in advance.

- Email is the best way to keep in touch so make sure yours is ready to use.

- Make sure you know about local customs – it might not be polite to wander around in bare feet or take photos of locals.

- Travel can be boring, so be sure to have a good book and plenty of music on your iPod!

- Try to learn a few phrases in the local language – that and a big smile and good attitude will get you far.

- Soft racks for the hire car are really useful, or just straps will do. Avoid showing hire car companies that you are going to load their car up with tons of boards.

Travel websites

- www.responsibletravel.com – 'holidays that give the world a break'.

- www.statravel.co.uk – for cheap, surfer-friendly insurance.

- www.fco.gov.uk – check the latest travel warnings and information about jabs you need.

- www.wannasurf.com – know where to go before you get there.

- www.surfinggb.com – lists BSA approved schools.

- www.bbc.co.uk/languages – brush up on the local language before you go.

- http://matadortravel.com – loads of travel articles.

'Try to learn a few phrases in the local language – that and a big smile and good attitude will get you far.'

Summing Up

Surfing and travel go together naturally, so even if you're skint you've got to try it! Cheap package holidays, late deals, going with a big group of friends, joining organised trips with college or university (many unis have great surf clubs) – there's always a way. And if you can afford a boat trip or dream destination like Hawaii, go for it! Either way, make sure you think about the impact of surf travel on the environment and respect the local culture while enjoying it to the max. Surf trips are holidays with a difference.

Chapter Seven

Mind, Body and Spirit

Surfing is a sport which requires a good basic level of fitness, and for safety's sake you should be able to swim 50m easily. Beyond that, the fitter and healthier you are the better your surfing will be. Paddling out in particular can be a struggle otherwise!

Just surfing on its own, getting out there in the waves, will increase your level of fitness amazingly. But there are other things you can do to really give yourself a boost in the waves, it doesn't have to mean hours in the gym. Pick things you like to do and you're more likely to stick to your fitness plan, reach your goals and surf stronger and longer!

Nutrition

There's lots of conflicting advice about what to eat and what not to eat these days, but if you stick to the basics you'll not go far wrong – make sure you get your five-a-day and cut down on high-fat, high-sugar, processed and convenience foods. A little bit of what you fancy won't hurt, but make sure you keep a balance. Moderate your alcohol intake and make sure you are hydrated – six to eight glasses of water (a couple of litres) a day is good, and fizzy drinks don't count! You need more in hot climates and if you're exercising loads. Our bodies are 70% water, so drinking plenty is one of the best things you can do to help your body work properly.

Carbohydrates are great for slow-release energy to keep you going during a surf and fill you up afterwards. Try some porridge for breakfast, a banana pre-surf and some pasta afterwards. In the UK, flasks of warm drinks are often essential too!

'Surfing is a sport which requires a good basic level of fitness, and for safety's sake you should be able to swim 50m easily.'

A good diet will keep your weight stable, gives you plenty of energy for your daily life as well as sport, keeps your complexion clear and your immune system and all organs functioning properly.

Yoga and surfing

Yoga is a discipline for body and mind which began in ancient India over 4,000 years ago. The word yoga means 'to bring together or unite' and refers to the linking of mind and body. Hatha yoga brings balance to mind and body through the practise of asanas (postures) and breathing (pranayama). There are actually six branches to yoga, but in the West the emphasis is generally placed on the postures.

So why is yoga so essential for surfing? Yoga is of benefit to everyone, surfer or not, of any age and fitness level. For surfing, it strengthens the body, improves flexibility, co-ordination and balance, and provides a good counterpoint to strenuous cardio training, also helping to prevent injury. It also helps with lung capacity and breathing, self discipline and maintaining calm in stressful situations like large waves. Many famous surfers from Kelly Slater to Serena Brooke are hooked on yoga. Yoga feels amazing to wake you up in the morning, is a good pre-surf warm-up, and is total bliss to realign and stretch out those tired muscles after a surf session.

There are different types of yoga, so if you prefer a strenuous practise that leaves you out of breath, you can try ashtanga or power yoga, or if you prefer to stretch deeply and think about the movement of every muscle, Iyengar might be for you. And there are loads of others in between!

The best way to learn and benefit from yoga is to find a good class with an experienced teacher. Classes last from one to two hours generally, and should always include a rest period at the end called savasana, a wonderful relaxing meditation. Some classes will focus on asanas only, some will include pranayama (breathing exercises).

'Yoga feels amazing to wake you up in the morning, is a good pre-surf warm-up, and is total bliss to realign and stretch out those tired muscles after a surf session.'

There are also loads of yoga books and DVDs on the market, and luckily for us, some of the very best ones are focused on surfing. Check out Peggy Hall's *Yoga for Surfers I, II and III*, *Surf Stronger Core Training 1 and 2*, featuring pro surfer girl Serena Brooke, and *Yoga for Boardsports*, another Peggy Hall production.

Swim training

There's nothing quite like surfing to train for surfing, and many pros will state that they do little else. However, in the UK it's not always possible to jump in the waves to train. Swimming is the next best thing. You can check out websites like www.swimplan.co.uk and get yourself a tailored programme, or talk to one of the swim coaches at your local pool. Hypoxic training, where you take fewer breaths, is excellent for surfing as it really builds your lung capacity. When it's warm enough, swimming in the sea is even better practise as you can learn more about the ocean around you and get used to swells.

Paddle training is also great, so when it's flat hop on a big board and paddle a mile, then turn and paddle back! This is a killer at first, so it's wonderful to see yourself going further and getting fitter.

'Hypoxic training, where you take fewer breaths, is excellent for surfing as it really builds your lung capacity.'

Surf simulation

Indo or balance boards have become the surfer's best friend in recent years. They're fun and easy to use, and will help you with balance, co-ordination and strength. You can even practise cross-stepping on it – but be careful! Indo boards are sold with DVDs of moves to try.

Pop-ups

Practising of your pop-ups on dry-land, even just five or 10 a day, can make a massive difference. Try it, especially if you're fluffing your takeoffs! Even pro surfers swear by this technique, you will see the benefit if you stick with it.

Cross-training

Running, cycling, rowing, riding, dancing and any other sports that get you breathless will all help with your cardiovascular fitness and as such, your surfing. Pick something you like and will stick to, and watch your surfing benefit. Cross-training means working out in different ways – running works you out differently to swimming, for example – and provides your body with a balanced all-round level of fitness.

If you are a gym bunny, get a personal trainer to build an all-round routine for you which focuses on your upper body strength. This is something that beginner surfers in particular have trouble with, and lack of upper body strength means difficulties paddling out and popping up. You also need strong legs to pull powerful turns, and a good level of cardio fitness, so try to use a wide range of machines in the gym.

'Running, cycling, rowing, riding, dancing and any other sports that get you breathless will all help with your cardiovascular fitness and as such, your surfing.'

Train your mind too!

The Surfer's Mind by Richard Bennett has already been mentioned. Bennett is the leading expert on surf psychology and his book will help you with positive strategies for everything from tackling bigger waves to competitive surfing. Even if you just want to surf for fun, it's worth a look. He talks about motivation, goal setting, attitude, confidence, dealing with life's up and downs, and so much more.

Resources

UK fitness guru Lee Stanbury has a new book out, called *The Complete Guide to Surf Fitness*. In it, he and Ben Skinner (champion longboarder) clearly present and demonstrate the moves that you need to get yourself surf fit. It's essential reading for anyone interested in boosting their performance.

Surf Flex by Paul Frediani, 'Flexibility, yoga and conditioning for the ultimate surfing experience!' Check this out for loads of balance board, Swiss ball and strength exercises. It's really in-depth and contains loads of advice from pro surfers too. There are routines for all levels of fitness.

Need2Know

13 ways to improve your surfing, mind and body

- Practice press-ups and pop-ups – upper body strength holds back many a surfer.

- Conditions – make sure you learn about the best conditions for your spots. Be in the right place at the right time (never an exact science).

- Read technique books and watch training DVDs.

- Visualising – replay your best moves, imagine the move you want to improve on.

- More coaching will definitely help, no question.

- Keeping a wave log/journal will remind you how much progress you're making.

- Friends who will push you (call you into waves, make you want to go for it and so on) are invaluable, and extra fun.

- Travel – something to look forward to, and you will definitely improve. Different beaches down the road or different countries, it's all good.

- Challenge – surf different breaks, push yourself out of your comfort zone.

- Equipment – you need the right board – this cannot be stressed enough.

- Video/photos – 'do I really look like that?!' Sadly, yes, but it'll help you improve to see it!

- DVDs – watch really good surfers. Watching real surfers in real waves down your local spot helps too.

- Don't surf – if you don't really want to surf today or you're not enjoying your surfing much in general – take a break. Injured surfers often find a break makes them super-keen to get back out there when they're ready.

Summing Up

■ Look after your health, train regularly and get practising! You'll start to notice the benefits and it'll help no end with your surfing.

■ Yoga is good for learning to control your breath and also very good for warming up and stretching afterwards.

■ Any kind of cardiovascular exercise is good for your fitness levels and swimming is excellent for keeping your fitness levels tip top for surfing.

Chapter Eight

Surf Culture

The contest scene

In the 1960s, surfers with a competitive bent wanted to test themselves year-round and began to loosely organise themselves to create a world tour. Check out Wayne 'Rabbit' Bartholomew's biography (see overleaf) for a fascinating insight into how this worked.

These days, the World Championship Tour, run by the Association of Surfing Professionals, is a worldwide, high profile, glamorous affair, with live web coverage of most events. Events are held at revered surf spots such as Teahupoo in Tahiti, J-Bay in South Africa and the famous Pipeline in Hawaii. There is a second tier of competitions which are designed to boost up and coming surfers into the elite tour; this is called the World Qualifying Series. There are also junior women's tour events. The pro-surfing year traditionally begins at Easter-time and ends with the Triple Crown events in Hawaii at the end of the year. Check out www.worldprosurfers.com and www.aspworldtour.com to see the latest info on the tours. The rankings and judging criteria for professional events are complicated to say the least – the best and most fun way to learn is to play fantasy surfer, www.fantasysurfer.com.

In the UK, there is currently a WQS event run at Thurso in Scotland, and one in Cornwall in the summertime – it's well-worth going to see the best surfers in the world if you can! Also in the UK, and more at the level of mere mortals, the UK Pro Surf Association runs a series of competitions known as the UK Pro Surf Tour around the UK and Ireland to decide the UK champions. The tour's website is at www.ukprosurf.com. Many surfers who succeed in events on this tour go on to compete in WQS events.

Books

There are tons of surfing books out now, from fiction to training manuals to beautiful coffee table books. Here's a small selection.

Travel Tales

Riding the Magic Carpet – Tom Anderson. An excellent look at the life of a wandering surfer, and written by a UK author.

Surf Nation – Alex Wade. Examines UK surf culture in detail.

Biography

Kelly Slater – For The Love. A close and fascinating look at the life of the best surfer ever.

MP – The Life of Michael Peterson, a radical Aussie surfer in the 70s.

Bustin Down the Door – Wayne 'Rabbit' Bartholomew's tale of the rise of competitive surfing.

'There are tons of surfing books out now, from fiction to training manuals to beautiful coffee table books.'

Art

Switchfoot – art, music, stoke, style and of course surf.

September – a collaborative project charting a winter chasing waves in Ireland.

Fiction

The Dogs of Winter, *Tapping the Source*, *Tijuana Straits* – Kem Nunn.

In Search of Captain Zero – Allan Weisbecker. A road trip and a search for a lost friend in Mexico.

Breath – Tim Winton. Set in Western Australia, a coming of age tale.

Spot guides

Surfing in the UK and Ireland, *Surfing in Europe* - Chris Nelson and Demi Taylor.

Wavefinder Guides – pocket sized, ideal for travel (see help list).

Stormrider Guides – the classic surf spot books (see help list).

History

The Surfing Tribe – Roger Mansfield. The first book to document the rise of surfing in Britain from the 1930s to the modern day. Detailed and fascinating. For more information on the rise of surfing in the UK check out www. museumofbritishsurfing.org.uk.

Magazines

- *CARVE surfing magazine* is the UK's best-selling surf mag.
- *SurfGirl* is the UK's only surf and lifestyle mag for girls.
- *Wavelength* is the UK's longest-running surf mag.
- *The Surfer's Path* contains more in-depth articles on a wide range of surfing themes.
- *Surf Europe* – fairly self-explanatory!
- *Surfer, Surfing* – the main American mags which you will see in the odd UK newsagent and airport shops.
- *ASL* and *Tracks* – the main Aussie mags, often very funny and slickly produced.

Websites

This is just a tiny selection of the many, many amazing surfing websites out there!

- www.a1surf.com – online community, forecasts, photos, webcams, shop, classifieds.
- www.wannasurf.com – spot guide, beware of people trying to feed false information!
- www.surfline.com – global surf forecasting and news.
- www.surfersvillage.com – tons of surfing news.
- www.extremepie.com – great online surf shop.
- www.surfinggb.com – UK governing body for surfing.
- www.worldprosurfers.com – sick coverage of the best surfers in the world.

DVDs

Some specific training DVDs like *Yoga for Surfers* have already been mentioned in the book. Here are a few other seminal surfing DVDs that you might like to check out.

Classics

Big Wednesday – a classic film, the tale of some conscript-dodging surfers in LA in the 70s.

Endless Summer I and II – the classic road trip surf flicks.

Morning of the Earth – a hippy, soulful cruising escape in the 70s.

Newer releases

There are loads of surf DVDs coming out all the time. Make sure you check out surf websites and Amazon reviews to get the type of thing you want. There's everything out there from hippy to razor-sharp cutting edge.

Modern Collective – new school surfers busting out the most progressive moves, this one was long-awaited and didn't disappoint.

Dude Cruise – classic surf flick format and amazing moves from three top surfers.

Lost Prophets – a spiritual regression to surfing's roots.

Searching for Michael Peterson – the story of Australia's biggest surfing cult hero, his surfing life and battle with drink, drugs and schizophrenia.

Summing Up

Phew! And this is just a personal selection of the surf media that's out there. Arm yourself with this book's glossary and immerse yourself in the amazing history and culture of the sport. Whether you prefer tales of Hawaiian history or the fast-paced live streaming of the ASP competitions, the best place to get initial information is the Internet. From there, you can pick and choose your own favourite aspects, personalities, destinations and inspirations.

Help List

A1 Surf

www.a1surf.com

An online surfing community, providing the latest surf reports, surf forecasts and UK surf news.

Association of Surfing Professional (ASP)

www.aspworldtour.com

Find out about the latest info on the tours.

BBC Languages

www.bbc.co.uk/languages

Brush up on the local language before your next beach holiday.

Easy Tide

http://easytide.ukho.gov.uk

Provides tidal data for over 7,000 ports worldwide, just click on 'predict' to access free predictions for the next seven days.

Ebay

www.ebay.co.uk

Find your dream second-hand surf board on Ebay (maybe).

Extreme Pie

www.extremepie.com

Online surf shop.

Fantasy Surfer

www.fantasysurfer.com

Much like fantasy football, except with surfers!

Foreign and Commonwealth Office (FCO)

www.fco.gov.uk
Find out about travel advice, warnings and where your local embassy will be when you go abroad.

Go Ireland

www.goireland.com
Information about surfing and tourism in Ireland.

Live Surf Cams

www.livesurfcams.co.uk
Have a look at your local breaks before you head down there.

Magicseaweed.co.uk

www.magicseaweed.co.uk
Find your nearest beach and see a rating for the surf in the coming week.

Matador Travel

http://matadortravel.com
Travel website where you can access loads of information and articles by other travellers.

Met Office

www.metoffice.gov.uk
The UK's weather service.

Museum of British Surfing

www.museumofbritishsurfing.org.uk
Based in North Devon, the Museum of British Surfing has collections of surfboards and paraphernalia from the ages of surfing.

Morocsurf.com

www.morocsurf.com
The first surf camp in Morocco, it's a family run business providing accommodation and surf lessons.

MPORA

www.mpora.com
A huge action sports community with lots of videos.

National Data Buoy Center

www.ndbc.noaa.gov
Find your nearest buoy. Look for the windspeed, dominant wave period (how far apart the waves are) and wave height readings. The site is US-based but you can find your nearest UK buoy on here.

Responsible Travel

www.responsibletravel.com
A leading travel agent for responsible holidays.

Royal National Lifeboat Institution (RNLI)

www.rnli.org.uk
A charity funded by voluntary donations. RNLI provide a 24-hour lifeboat search and rescue service around the coasts of the UK and Ireland, as well as a seasonal lifeguard service on many of the busiest beaches.

Seabase

www.seabase.ltd.uk
An online shop selling everything you'll need to get going plus custom-made surfboards.

Second-hand Boards

www.second-handboards.com
A dedicated second-hand surfboard directory. The service offers users two options: search for boards in their area, or upload their own boards onto the website absolutely free of charge.

STA Travel

www.statravel.co.uk
Find cheap flights, accommodation and round-the-world ticket deals with STA Travel.

Stormrider Guides

www.lowpressure.co.uk

Publishers of surf travel guide books for locations around the world.

Surfers Against Sewage (SAS)

www.sas.org.uk

SAS campaign for clean, safe recreational waters, free from sewage effluents, toxic chemicals, marine litter and nuclear waste. SAS also campaign to protect surf spots from environmental damage, negative impacts on wave quality and to safeguard recreational water users right of access.

Surfing GB

www.surfinggb.com

The BSA promotes surfing and represents the interests of all surfers in Great Britain and the Channel Islands.

Surfline

www.surfline.com

Global surf forecasting and news.

Surf Maroc

www.surfmaroc.co.uk

A Morocco-based surf holiday company.

Surfers Village

www.surfersvillage.com

Tons of surfing news.

Swim Plan

www.swimplan.com

Improve your fitness with a free personalised swimming training plan.

Tiger 24

www.tiger24.com

A webcam site where you can select from various webcams to see the surf before you head down the beach.

UK Pro Surf Tour

www.ukpsa.org.uk
Information on the UK Pro Surf Tour can be found here.

Wanna Surf

www.wannasurf.com
Spot guide website with information on destinations all over the world.

Wavefinder

www.wave-finder.com
Publisher of action sports travel guides and technique manuals, specialising in surf, snow and bike sports.

Wave Watch

www.wavewatch.com
A webcam site with cameras based in the US and Hawaii.

Wind Guru

www.windguru.com
A specialised tool to help forecasting weather for surfers.

World Pro Surfers

www.worldprosurfers.com
Information on pro surfers, photos, videos and tours.

XC Weather

www.xcweather.co.uk
Another specialised tool to help forecasting weather for surfers.

Glossary

The mainstream media more often than not sound totally ridiculous when they portray surfing — this is because it has its own language which is constantly developing and changing. What was cool a few years ago won't be now, so pay attention to the surf mags and websites if you don't want to sound like a 'kook'!

Aerial or Air
A manoeuvre where the surfer's board leave the surface of the water.

A-Frame
A peak with both a left and a righthand wave breaking at either side at the same time, thus making it look like a letter A.

Alaia
Old wooden surfboard used in ancient Hawaii.

Aloha
Hawaiian greeting word which also means peace, good wishes, welcome.

Backdoor
Taking off behind the peak (harder than taking off on the peak). Good for getting into the barrel.

Backing off
When a wave breaks or begins to break and then hits deeper water and fattens out. Frustrating!

Bail
Leaving the board and diving under waves.

Barrel
Surfing's nirvana. A hollow tube of a wave formed when the lip pitches out and forms a cavern that a skilled surfer can tuck themselves inside of.

Bathymetry
The measurement of depths of water in oceans, seas, and lakes. The topography of the ocean floor or underwater bottom.

Beachbreak
A wave that breaks over a sandy bottom.

Blank
A hunk of foam that will be shaped by a shaper into a surfboard.

Blown out
Really onshore, windy and messy, pretty much unsurfable.

Bodyboard
A short squarish board with no fins in it, ridden lying down with swimfins often attached to the feet. Also known as a lid, mat, sponge and many other slightly derogatory terms!

Bomb
A bigger or better wave than those that have gone before in a session.

Bonzer
A surfboard with a five-fin setup, created in the 70s by the Campbell brothers.

Carve
A long drawn-out and powerful turn which slices into the wave.

Clean
Either no wind or a light offshore produces clean conditions, where there is no chop on the face of the wave. Ideal.

Close out
Where a wave breaks top to bottom all along its length. Also known as a straighthander, because you cannot surf along the face.

Concave
A dip shaped into the bottom of a board to increase speed. Usually between the fins, sometimes at the nose.

Cooking
Often followed by 'bru', a South African favourite term for great waves.

Cowabunga
Please, do not use this…it's an old and now unused (except by mainstream media) term rather like a surfing war cry. Cringe-worthy.

Cranking
Sick (excellent) waves. You can also crank a turn, i.e. turn powerfully.

Cutback
A series of turns made to return a surfer to the power pocket, right at the peak of the wave.

Dawn Patrol
Early morning surf session.

Ding
Damage to a surfboard.

Double up
When two waves combine to form a larger wave, or when they don't quite combine and thus neither is surfable.

Down-the-line
The direction a surfer surfs in, from the starting point on the shoulder along the clean face.

Drilling
Getting a kicking from a wave or a set. You can be drilled right into the sand if you're unlucky!

Drop in
A surfer who takes off and gets in the way of another surfer who is closer to the peak has dropped in.

Dude
Californian term meaning surfer, cool guy, man. A bit clichéd over here!

Elephant Gun
Or more commonly just a gun. A large board for large waves.

Epoxy
A type of plastic resin used by some manufacturers in place of polyester resin.

Face
The unbroken front part of the wave - the blue part you can see.

Fetch
The area across the ocean over which a wind with a consistent direction

generates waves and sea state.

Fin
The pointy things on the bottom of the board… They dig into the wave and give the board directional hold.

Firing.
Going off. Really good surf.

Fish
A shorter, fatter, rounder shape in general with a wide nose, designed to make the most of small waves. A plethora of options from retro to cutting-edge shapes.

Flat
No surfable waves in sight. Bad.

Floater
A manoeuvre where the surfer slides along on top of a broken section of a wave.

Forehand/frontside
Surfing facing the wave, i.e. righthanders if you are regular-footed and lefthanders if you are goofy.

Fullsuit
A wetsuit which covers the whole body.

Glass job
Final coating of fibreglass cloth and resin given to a new surfboard.

Glassy
Even cleaner than clean. Good!

Gnarly
Heavy, scary situation or waves. Slightly cliched now.

Goat boat
Surf ski, canoe or other unwieldy sit-down craft that should not be anywhere near surfers.

Going off
Really good surf.

Goofy foot
Surfing right foot forward.

Green Room
An old-fashioned term for the barrel.

Grommet
A young surfer.

Groundswell
Waves that have been generated far away and thus have a high period (10 seconds or more). Clean, powerful and the best for surfing.

Hang Five
A longboarding manoeuvre where the surfer puts five toes over the end of the nose of the surfboard.

Hang Ten
10 toes over the nose. Hard.

Heavy
Powerful waves which will give you a good hiding.

Hollow
Barrelling conditions.

Impact zone
Right where the waves are breaking, and right where you don't want to be caught.

Inside
To be caught inside is to be too close to the beach when a set unloads, giving you a thrashing. The inside is where the waves are breaking.

Jack up
When a wave rears up quickly in height because it has just hit shallower water.

Keg
Another word for a barrel.

Kick out
A manoeuvre to end the wave, basically a top turn out through the lip and off the back of the wave. A flying kick out is a more showy version.

Kook
Bad surfer.

Layback
A turn where the fins are released and the surfer almost falls off the back but is pushed upright by the whitewater.

Leash
A urethane cord and Velcro contraption which attaches board to surfer. Pretty essential in these crowded days.

Leash plug
A small plug in the tail of the deck of a board with a bar to attach a leash string to.

Legrope
Or 'leggie'. Another name for a leash. Common term in Australia.

Line up
Where surfers sit and wait for waves, just outside of where they will break.

Lip
The edge of the wave just as it's beginning to break.

Log
Longboard.

Longboard
A board over eight feet for cruising and walking (cross-stepping). Longboards can be old-school, but there are now many progressive shapes that will pull some amazing moves.

Loose
A board that is easy to throw around in the waves. Often with two fins or a quad setup.

Lull
A period of relative calm between sets of waves. Ideal to paddle out in, or just catch your breath.

Lumpy
Literally, bumps and swells in the wave which make it harder to judge and ride the swell.

Macker
A big wave. 'Macking' can be used to describe a big swell.

Mal
Longboard. A Malibu board is a longboard design that came out of California.

Messy
Choppy, onshore, confused conditions. Not clean. Harder to surf, but often still plenty of fun.

Mushy
Weak, small mushburgers are not good waves. Little energy, usually from windswells.

Neoprene
Stretchy rubber made from melted down and moulded petroleum chips. Made up of lots of little insulating cells to keep you toasty.

Nose
Front of a surfboard.

Noseguard
A protective hard rubber tip often used to protect the board and soft body parts.

Offshore
When the breeze blows from the land out to sea. Cleans the wave faces up and makes for good rides (when not too strong, when it can be difficult to paddle into).

Off the lip
A top turn performed sharply at the top of the wave in the lip area.

Onshore
When the wind is blowing from the sea onto the land. Generally makes for messy surf.

Outside
Further out to sea. A cry of 'Outside' means the same as 'Heads up! Waves coming!'

Over the falls
Wiping out from the top of the wave and falling to the bottom.

Overhead
A wave that is taller than the surfer riding it. Often used rather than arbitrary feet to measure wave height.

Pearl
Where the nose of the board pushes or catches the wave and stalls. Often results in a wipeout or fluffed takeoff.

Peeling
A wave breaking perfectly from one end to the other all the way down the line.

Pigdog
Crouching low and grabbing the rail of a surfboard when going backside to hold in the barrel or tube.

Pop up
Getting to your feet on a surfboard.

Pin tail
A tail shape which comes to a point. Often used on big wave boards to help them turn.

Pull in
Turning tight to get into the barrel.

Pumping
Going off; excellent surf, strong swell.

Quad
A board with four fins, two on each side. Looser to surf.

Quiver
A collection of surfboards.

Rail
The edges of a surfboard, which it turns on.

Re-entry
Performing a top turn followed dropping down with the whitewater.

Regular foot
Surfing left foot forward.

Resin
A liquid plastic that sets hard when mixed with MEKP. Used to seal a shaped blank and repair dings.

Reverse Vee
The opposite of a concave in the bottom of a board, i.e. convex.

Rhino Chaser
Old-fashioned term for a gun, a big-wave board.

Rip (current or tide)
A strong pull of water.

Reo
See re-entry.

SAS
Surfers Against Sewage, the UK pollution group. See www.sas.org.uk.

Set
A group of waves, usually from two to nine waves together. The legendary seventh and/or ninth waves are supposed to be the biggest and best…

Shacked
Getting barrelled.

Shaper
Surfboard maker.

Shorebreak
Or 'shorey'. A line of waves breaking right on the beach which must be tackled before paddling out. Can be fun to ride, can also hurt! Often found at high tide.

Shoulder
The unbroken part of the wave that the surfer surfs on.

Shredding
Surfing powerfully and technically.

Sick
Really, really good.

Skeg
Fin.

Slop
Messy, weak, low period surf.

Slotted
Barrelled. Yes, there are a lot of words for this!

Snap
A fast sharp turn.

Snake
Paddling around other surfers to take pole position for waves. Bad manners.

Sneaker set
Unexpectedly large set during a session which tends to take out the entire lineup.

Spray
Water thrown up by the fins as a surfer slices into the wave. Good.

Spin out
Losing the tail during a manoeuvre when the fins slide out.

Square tail
A tail shape that looks…square. A good all round and popular choice.

Stick
Surfboard.

Stoked
Surfed-out and happy. Do not over-use unless you are from California.

Stringer
A line of wood running up the middle of a surfboard blank for strength and symmetry. One stringer is the most common, but you can have more.

Swallow tail
A tail shaped like a swallow's wing or W.

Switch foot
Someone who can surf both ways around, i.e. goofy and natural.

Tail
The rear of a surfboard.

Take off
The start of a ride where the surfer paddles and pops up.

Thruster
The three-fin surfboard popularised by Simon Anderson in the 80s.

Tombstoning
When the surfer is deep underwater and their board is pulled by the leash until it sticks up like a tombstone out of the water.

Tube
Barrel.

Twin fin
A board with two fins. Loose and quite retro.

Wahine
Hawaiian term for a female surfer.

Wax
Sticky substance rubbed on the deck of the board to give grip.

Wedge
Where two waves come together and the size is magnified. Bodyboarders love this.

Windswell
Smaller, poor waves generated by local winds and thus without the organisation or power of groundswell.

Wipeout
Falling off.

Zipperless
A wetsuit made with any arrangement of flaps and Velcro rather than zips, which let water in.

Zoo
A crowded line up.

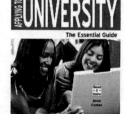
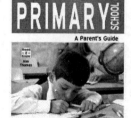

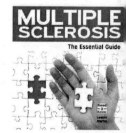